$afe Money Matters

FINDING SAFE HARBOR

IN A STORM-FILLED WORLD

$afe Money Matters

FINDING SAFE HARBOR
IN A STORM-FILLED WORLD

Brad Pistole, President & CEO
Trinity Insurance and Financial
Services, Inc.

5511 N. Farmer Branch Rd.
Suite 101-106
Ozark, Missouri 65721
417.581.9222
www.guaranteedsafemoney.com
KSGF 104.1 FM *Safe Money Radio*

Expert Press

www.ExpertPress.net

Copyright

Permission to reproduce or transmit in any form or by any means, electronic or mechanical, including photocopying and recording, or by an information storage and retrieval system, must be obtained by contacting the author through his website.

ISBN-13: 978-1502720252

ISBN-10: 1502720256

This book is for educational purposes with the sole intent to educate the reader. By writing this book, the author is not giving legal advice. The author does not have any knowledge of the reader's specific situation; therefore, readers should consult with a professional before acting on any of the information contained in this book. The author has taken reasonable precautions in the writing of this book and believes the facts presented in the book are accurate as of the date it was written. However, the author specifically disclaims any liability resulting from the use or application of the information in this book. If you need professional assistance, you should seek the services of a competent professional.

First Printing: October 2014

Second Printing: February 2017

Dedication

This book is dedicated to my dad, Joe Pistole,
who has spent his entire life working in the insurance
and financial services industry.
Your knowledge, character and commitment to always
doing what is best for your clients, friends and family
have made me who I am today.
Thank you for believing in me and for teaching me the
things that matter most in this life and in the life to come.

Acknowledgements

Special thanks to Nate Murphree, my good friend and fellow advisor who helped me from day one when I started my business in 2008. He has been with me every single step of the way, and I wouldn't be where I am today without his help, advice and support. The team at FIRST ANNUITY in Denver, Colorado is like family to me. I am thankful for all of you.

Special thanks to Ed Slott and Company, LLC. I am blessed to have worked with Ed as an Ed Slott Master Elite Advisor for several years now, and I wouldn't trade that relationship and knowledge for anything. Ed, you are simply THE BEST! (www.irahelp.com)

I am blessed to have the two most amazing kids in this world! Autumn and Hunter, you make everything I do worthwhile. I love you both!

Testimonials and Customer Reviews

My wife and I responded to Brad's invitation to attend his "Financial Planning Seminar." He presented profound information on "Fixed Indexed Annuities." It was an excellent presentation that evening.

We wanted to get out of the Market, especially my wife, because of the risks involved. We moved here from California, and began looking for a local investor. After attending many seminars we discovered that Brad Pistole met our needs.

We met with Brad at least four meetings, where he graciously gave of his time answering all of our concerns. After feeling confident in him, we moved a substantial amount of money from the Market with Brad's recommendation to a "Fixed Indexed Annuity."

As we are in our seventies, we feel comfortable with our decision and my wife has had the best night's sleep she has had in a long time.

We are also pleased after spending time with Brad to know that he operates a "Faith Based Business."

Jim & Ruth Roberts

Ozark, Missouri

Since first meeting Brad, we have been more impressed by his financial knowledge than by any other financial advisor we have ever met. We are also impressed with his thoroughness in presenting the benefits of annuities. We feel he goes out of his way to take care of us as clients. And one of the main things we like is his prompt manner of keeping appointments.

We had been in the market 100% for many years, but now, at our ages, with the uncertainty of the market, we feel much more at ease with Brad and his annuities.

We would urge anyone to sit down with Brad to let him show you the tools he uses to ensure the safety of your funds. We trust him implicitly and feel very secure with the programs he represents.

He is the most efficient, pleasant and knowledgeable person we have ever dealt with in the financial arena.

Hugh & Clara Kirkland

Age 82 & 77

Springfield, Missouri

In 2010 we would listen to "Safe Money Radio" as we returned home from church on Sunday mornings. After several weeks, I knew I needed more information about this financial plan that sounded too good to be true. The first meeting with Brad exceeded all expectations. His honesty and integrity were evident. We have placed our trust and confidence in Brad as he has guided and informed us down a secure financial pathway. He has not let us down. We just wish we had learned about Brad and "Safe Money Radio" two years earlier!

Phyllis Fennell

Nixa, Missouri

With the uncertain financial market, I had been looking for a more stable financial base to diversify some of my holdings. I first heard Brad on a local radio station and was so impressed that I ordered his package of information by mail. After reading his book and materials, I called Brad and my wife and I met with him. I was very impressed with Brad's presentation, solutions and the safety his plan offered our retirement savings.

I was so impressed that I called my brother and asked him to go back with me to meet with Brad. Brad's programs have given both of our families a sense of peace and less stress. He is always available and returns our calls promptly. His knowledge of IRA's and financial programs and his honesty and faith make him not only our advisor, but someone we are proud to call a friend.

James Y. Fairbairn

Springfield, MO

Comments from Other Trinity Clients

"I am glad you came into my life. Now I don't have to worry anymore. I can sleep at night knowing my money is safe and I don't have to follow the market every day."

"I had my savings in three different money markets, which wasn't making very much interest at all. Then I heard the Safe Money Radio program and moved my accounts. I just received my first annual report. My interest for the year was twice the amount I would have received from the bank. The value of my investments never goes down. That is very important to me. The market has been so unstable lately. I know my funds will always be there when I need it."

"Brad's Financial Planning Seminar was a life changing experience for us. We had so many things that needed to be done after we retired and he helped us every step of the way. Thank you for finding us."

"My decision to get out of the stock market and out of risk at age 70 could not have come at a better time. Brad helped me develop a complete estate plan and it has given my family financial security and peace of mind."

Introduction

When I first started my financial planning business, I read every book I could get my hands on even though I had already acquired a vast amount of knowledge from my dad. I attended an endless number of online webinars and many public seminars and conferences led by "professional advisors" with impressive credentials and reputations. They all gave what was essentially the same advice, and I drew one extremely important conclusion very quickly. As Will Rogers once said,

> "It isn't what we don't know that gives us trouble, it's what we know that ain't so."

In other words, as you may have heard me say on the radio and in my retirement planning courses, "If you do what everyone else does, you're going to get what everyone else is getting." And that's *not* good when it comes to retirement planning and your peace of mind.

Why? What exactly is everyone else getting? Research says that 60% of all retired individuals will fail, meaning they'll run out of money and be forced to go back to work during their retirement based on their current financial plan[i]. Typically, this financial plan is based on (bad) professional advice.

I've concluded, after talking to literally thousands of individuals across the country, that up to 90% of retirees in this great country are *not* getting security and peace of mind when they retire. Even at the outset of my financial planning career, I didn't have to be a rocket scientist to determine that the current system for investing and retiring in this country is broken—and in desperate need of repair.

That's why, for years, I've used my own methods for my clients (and for myself and my family)—with exceptional results. These methods are completely different from what you've probably heard from your broker and even from the professional celebrities on TV and radio. But remember, if you want to get the exact same results that everyone else is getting—if you *want* to risk being in the 60% of retirees whose financial plans result in failure—then simply keep doing what everyone else does. Go mainstream and be part of the crowd.

But if you want to be different, if you want an absolutely proven plan for success, and if you want to feel safe and secure about your financial future, then keep reading. I will share with you some of the ways our peace-of-mind planning will help provide the results you want for your retirement, and I will show you how to get more information about what we do for clients for a complete, safe financial plan.

Table of Contents

CHAPTER

1

BORN TO PLAN

You could say I was born to be a financial planner. I grew up in a financial planner's home, and it seems like I started learning about the importance of financial planning around the time I learned to talk. If you've heard me on the radio, you probably know that my dad has over 45 years of experience in the financial services industry as an agent and advisor. The last 17 years of his career were spent as a Merrill Lynch Assistant Vice President. He has his CLU (Chartered Life Underwriter) and several other licenses that allow him to represent his clients with a full-line of financial services. Now, at age 72, he is using his expertise to assist my company with safe financial planning.

Although I grew up in a financial expert's home and picked up a lot of his knowledge just by listening, my personal experience with finances began in a completely different way from my father's. My personal experience also began much later in my life than you might expect.

I began my journey after serving as a full-time minister for 17 years. Prior to ministry, I traveled an uncertain path with my own finances. At the tender age of 19, I was faced with the decision every minister has to make. Should I pay into the Social Security system or choose to create my own retirement account? (Most people don't realize their ministers have this option.) Older and wiser ministers advised me against paying into the system, assuring me that I could be a better steward of my money than the government.

Unfortunately, I (like most ministers) needed every penny I earned to make ends meet. I failed to contribute the money that would have gone to Social Security into a retirement account. Since the church didn't have a retirement plan, I had no retirement security whatsoever. Nothing! Fortunately, I realized the importance of saving by the time I was 27, and I opened an IRA account. It was very small, only a modest beginning, but at least I opened the account while I was still in my 20s.

Then at the age of 36, life happened. I found myself going through a divorce and suddenly I was the single, full-time parent of two teenagers. I had no Social Security and very little retirement. That sounds like it could have been bad news, possibly even catastrophic. But, as things turned out, the whole situation was a blessing in disguise.

My teenagers are wonderful kids and I love them. I have loved and appreciated being the primary influence in their lives. And I took my thirst for knowledge and my passion for helping people and decided to make a complete career change. Now, ten years later, I am blessed to be the president and CEO of a multimillion-dollar financial services company that is centered on customer service and caring for families and their financial futures. I have been so blessed to work with Ed Slott, America's IRA Expert, from 2010-2017. I am listed on Ed's Website, www.irahelp.com, as a Master Elite IRA Advisor. I have also been blessed to work with some of the best financial minds in the world through my partnership with MDRT. I have been recognized as a member of The Million Dollar Round Table—"The Premier Association of Financial Professionals"—from 2011-2017. And I was honored as a TOP of the TABLE producer in 2015, 2016 and 2017. I personally understand what the lack of a good retirement plan will eventually mean for a family, and I don't want anyone to experience that. So I have made it my passion to teach other people how to do whatever is necessary to secure their financial future and live the life they have always dreamed of.

CHAPTER

2

WHY I WROTE THIS BOOK

I wrote this book because I care about retirees and the 9,500 people or so who are retiring every day, who are worried about having enough money to last them through their retirement years. I don't want them to have to work when they're 80 or 90 years old just to make ends meet. I reach many people through my radio shows and through the retirement planning courses I teach at my office and on the campus of local universities, and I have a large client base, but there are still many of you out there who don't know that there *is* a way to protect your money from market fluctuations and taxes. In this book, I want to share that information with you so you can feel secure and have peace of mind. I want to reach a larger audience, as many of you as possible.

I want to talk to you if you're one of the millions still in your 50s or 60s who might be contributing to a 401(k) and getting your company's matching contribution. Right now, you probably don't realize that you're in a partnership with Uncle Sam. You have entered in an agreement, whether you realize it or not, that will require you to start taking taxable required minimum distributions (RMD) at age 70 1/2. Remember, those contributions were tax-*deferred*, not tax-free.

I want to talk to you if you're just getting ready to retire or if you've retired already, whether you've reached 70 1/2 or not, and if you have any type of tax-deferred retirement account, such as an IRA, 401k, 403b, TSP, etc. Because no matter which group you're in, you're likely to be looking at that those accounts and wondering, "Is there enough money in there to last the rest of my life?"

Some financial planners and companies will say you can answer that with a rule of thumb called the "4% withdrawal rule." It says you can withdraw 4% of your money in the first year of retirement, adjust the percentage for inflation each year thereafter, and your retirement money will last about 30 years. Well, rules of thumb can't always be relied upon.

Let me give you an example. I'm on the radio several times a week on a couple of different stations, and the thing callers say most often is that my methods are "just too good to be true" or "I wish I'd heard your program 10 years ago. How do I stop the bleeding?" One of these callers was a gentleman named Bob, who had invested his entire 401(k) in the stock market on the advice of a financial planner.

In 2004, Bob had retired in his mid-50s with over $600,000 in his account. He started taking distributions based on the 4% withdrawal rule of thumb. Then the stock market plummeted in 2008 and his 401(k) suddenly lost 40% of its value. Not only that, but he had been taking distributions and paying fees to his advisor. When he heard my program after he'd been retired for only four years, his 401(k) was down to $320,000—slightly more than half of what he'd started with, expecting it to last 30 years. He was down to fifty percent of his retirement money with potentially 87% of his "Golden Years" remaining. Suddenly that 4% rule of thumb wasn't looking too reliable.

Bob called into my program and asked what I could do for him. I won't go into complete detail here—that's what the rest of the book is about—but I will give you a snapshot so you understand how this works. After showing Bob my plan, he took all of his money out of the stock market. I put it into a three different "bucket" system, each bucket guaranteed not to lose principal no matter what happens in the stock market. The first bucket, called a SPIA (Single Premium Immediate Annuity) allowed Bob to continue receiving the same monthly income he was currently taking from his retirement plan. (Actually, we increased it by $50.00 a month.) In the other two buckets, we secured his future need for income by setting up annuities that have Lifetime Income Benefit Riders (LIBR) attached to the accounts. These riders pay a contractual guaranteed amount of money into the annuity account for a stated period of time. After five years, when the money from Bob's SPIA (bucket number #1) has been depleted, the money from bucket #2 will start to pay out. Because of the contractual guaranteed growth for five years with no risk of principal loss, the payout from bucket #2 will give Bob a pay *raise* after five years, which he'll need due to inflation.

Oh yeah, don't forget about bucket #3. During the ten years when the money from the first two buckets is used for distributions, bucket #3 is receiving tax-deferred, compounded, guaranteed growth. When Bob turns it on for income, his monthly check will be substantially higher than it was when he started the program. And what is the best part, you ask? The LIBR (Lifetime Income Benefit Rider) that is attached to his annuity guarantees that Bob can *never* run out of money when he starts taking his payment from bucket #3. No matter what happens in the market. No matter how long he lives. He will always have money because he has invested in an insured, guaranteed pension account that is guaranteed to pay him for life!

And that's why I wrote this book. I want to help more people get off the rollercoaster ride of market ups and downs, worrying about whether they'll have enough money to last their lifetime. I hate seeing or hearing from people who are literally scared to death that they'll wind up penniless or trying to find work in their 70s, 80s or even 90s because their money ran out. That doesn't have to happen.

You've worked hard, you've saved, you deserve to have peace of mind. I want to show you how to achieve it.

Brad Pistole, President and CEO
Trinity Insurance and Financial Services
417.581.9222
www.guaranteedsafemoney.com

3

THE #1 FEAR

RUNNING OUT OF MONEY BEFORE RUNNING OUT OF LIFE

In case you haven't been paying attention for the past 10 years, the internet, radio, TV and magazines have all been announcing that the number one fear of retirees is running out of money before they run out of life. No one wants to *have* to go back to work after retirement simply to make ends meet. I often ask my radio listeners and students in my college retirement planning courses to consider this, "If you don't believe this is a real possibility, think about how many 80-year-olds have greeted you at Walmart in the past month."

As I mentioned in the introduction, research suggests that 60% of all retirements today end in failure, with retirees returning to work to make ends meet. That is the number one fear that motivates seniors in planning for their future retirement. *No one* wants to experience this. To avoid this in your personal retirement plan, I'd like to ask you a few questions, beginning with this one; "Have you ever needed to stop and ask for directions?"

BAD DIRECTIONS AT A HIGH PRICE

Men often need directions, but seldom ask for them—it's just the way we're wired, isn't it? We always think we'll find the right way on our own, and we think that we'll find what we've been looking for right around the next corner.

I'm sure all of us have frustrating and probably equally entertaining stories about a time when we've been lost. I mean truly lost. Do you remember what that feels like? Maybe you headed in a certain direction for quite a while, convinced you were headed in the right direction, only to discover it wasn't the right direction at all. Then you realize you've wasted, or "lost," your time, your gas, your money and even part of your sanity—and now you'll have to start all over again and go in a completely different direction to reach your intended destination. Unfortunately, bad directions can sometimes result in taking the wrong turns in *life*.

Recently I needed several new photos for a website I was about to launch, so my assistant made an appointment for me with a professional photographer. She gave me the date and time and other information. On my way to the photographer's, it dawned on me that I had no idea where the studio was in the mall, and it's a pretty big mall. I called the mall's main number and asked customer service exactly where the store was located so I wouldn't waste time walking all over the place.

You know what's coming, don't you? I received a short set of directions that I trusted to be accurate. Ten minutes before my appointment I parked my vehicle outside near the entrance they said to use and headed into the mall. About five minutes into my search, I realized the directions weren't exactly right. The studio was nowhere to be found. I stopped in a store and asked someone who actually worked in the mall for better directions.

She graciously pointed me in the right direction. I followed the directions exactly, thinking that surely someone who works in the mall would give me accurate directions. Unfortunately, again, the directions weren't even close. I finally called my assistant, got the studio's number, and had them tell me exactly where they were. Altogether, I walked around the mall for almost 20 minutes and was 10 minutes late for my appointment.

Has this ever happened to you? Have you ever found yourself lost because of directions someone else gave you? Probably so.

Most of us, at some point in our lives, have been lost. Sometimes, at least in retrospect, it can be entertaining.

But it's no laughing matter when it comes to your retirement. I can't tell you how many phone calls I've received from truly distressed listeners to my radio program who have said, "I've done exactly what my broker has told me to do for the past 10 years and I'm not even close to my retirement goals." Many of you who have listened or who are reading right now can relate to their pain. Many of you were told exactly what to do by your brokers. You trusted them and paid them really well for their advice. You did as they advised and invested in the stock market—you followed their road map—and now you're worse off than when you started your retirement account. What went wrong?

BETTER DIRECTIONS AT NO COST

Let me ask you a question. Do you think you should pay someone for their directions and advice when they lose your money? If your answer is no, then we agree. I think it's time for you to get better advice, from someone who specializes in income retirement planning. Over the years, I've *never charged nor lost one penny* of my clients' money. Should I repeat that? I've never charged my clients for my advice and expertise, and my advice has never resulted in my clients losing one penny of their money. I help manage millions and millions of dollars and I specialize in Safe Money accounts that only go up in value. They do not go backwards; the balances do not go down, unless you reach in and take the money out yourself.

It doesn't matter what the stock market does; it cannot affect your retirement account. If this sounds interesting to you, let me ask you six very important questions.

1. Do you, or a family member you love, have a retirement account?

2. Has that retirement account lost some of its value in the recent past and left you discouraged?

3. If you could add up to 10% to that account's value right now, and *never lose* that gain, would you be interested in doing that?

4. If you could double your current account value in ten years, guaranteed, without question, would you do it?

5. Would you like to have guarantees for your retirement account so that it never loses another penny? It goes up when the market gains and the index rises, but it never goes down when the market declines and takes a loss?

6. Would you like to know that you and your spouse could have a guaranteed income stream from your retirement accounts that you could never outlive, no matter how long you live? Even if monthly pension payments from the account reduced your account balance to zero?

I know this sounds too good to be true because callers to my radio program tell me so. But it is true. If you answered yes to any of those six questions, you need to keep reading.

CHAPTER

4

THE SEVEN BIGGEST RETIREMENT MISTAKES

THE POWER OF HABITS

I'd like to begin with a story about a wise teacher who took his pupil for a stroll in the woods. Stopping before a tiny seedling, he instructed the pupil to pull it up. The boy did so easily. "Now pull up that one," said the teacher, indicating a more established sapling that reached up to the boy's knees. With a little effort, the boy yanked it up by the roots.

"Now this one," said the teacher, nodding to a more developed evergreen that was as tall as the boy.

With great effort, throwing all his weight and strength into the task and using a stick he found to prop the stump and roots, the boy finally got the tree loose and pulled it out of the ground.

Now the wise teacher said, "I would like you to pull up this last one."

The pupil followed the teacher's gaze, which fell upon a mighty oak, so tall the boy could barely see its top. Knowing the great struggle he'd recently undergone pulling up the much smaller tree, he simply told the teacher,

"I'm sorry, but I can't do that. It's impossible."

The teacher replied, "My son, you have just demonstrated the power that habits will have over your entire life."

The older they are, they bigger and more invincible they seem. The deeper their roots extend, the harder they are to pull up. Some habits grow so large, with roots so deep, you might even hesitate to *try* to change them. You see, we are what we repeatedly do. Webster's dictionary defines habits this way, "Something that a person does often and in a regular and repeated way. It is an acquired motive (purposeful) behavior that has become *nearly* or *completely involuntary*."

THE SEVEN BIGGEST MISTAKES

When it comes to the seven biggest retirement mistakes you can make, you might find it interesting to know that they have very little, if anything, to do with investing. They really have more to do with your habits and the choices you make on a daily basis. The seven biggest retirement mistakes are as follows:

1. Not contributing regularly to your retirement accounts.
2. Leaving your job and taking Social Security too soon.
3. Making required distribution mistakes.
4. Making the wrong rollover moves.
5. Falling prey to scams such as questionable or risky retirement transactions.
6. Failing to plan for taxes to make your retirement tax-efficient.
7. Working with the wrong financial advisor.

I could honestly write an entire book about these seven mistakes and how your financial habits affect these daily decisions. I will discuss them very briefly here.

To begin, let me ask you a question:

> If I offered you either one million dollars or one penny a day that would double every day for the next 31 days, which would you choose? If you are like most people and you start doing the math in your head, you're probably going to take the million dollars and RUN!

After 24 days, you would only have a little more than $83,000, with less than one week to go. But if you take the $1 million, you would lose out on *millions*. That's right, *millions*. Take a look at the chart below to see what happens in the last seven days. Maybe this will help you better understand the importance of starting early and contributing regularly to your retirement accounts, especially if they are protected against losses and fees.

Day 1:	$.01
Day 2:	$.02
Day 3:	$.04
Day 4:	$.08
Day 5:	$.16
Day 6:	$.32
Day 7:	$.64
Day 8:	$1.28
Day 9:	$2.56
Day 10:	$5.12
Day 11:	$10.24

Day 12:	$20.48
Day 13:	$40.96
Day 14:	$81.92
Day 15:	$163.84
Day 16:	$327.68
Day 17:	$655.36
Day 18:	$1,310.72
Day 19:	$2,621.44
Day 20:	$5,242.88
Day 21:	$10,485.76
Day 22:	$20,971.52
Day 23:	$41,943.04
Day 24:	$83,886.08
Day 25:	$167,772.16
Day 26:	$335,544.32
Day 27:	$671,088.64

Day 28:	$1,342,177.28
Day 29:	$2,684,354.56
Day 30:	$5,368,709.12
Day 31:	$10,737,418.24

Albert Einstein has often been credited with saying, "The greatest invention of all time is compounded interest." I often quote Ed Slott, and one of my favorite Ed Slott sayings is, "It's not how much you *make*, it's how much you *keep* that counts." The bottom line is this: start early, contribute often, and make *wise* investment choices. It could be the difference between $1 million and $10,737,418.24.

How many Social Security Workshop invitations have you received in the mail this week? If you're over the age of 50, it's probably a dozen or more. As you may or may not know, there are over 500 different ways to file for Social Security. There are over 80 different specific combinations for married couples to file. Does it really matter? *Yes!* It matters, if your *lifetime income* matters to you.

How you file and *when* you file can make a difference of more than $150,000 in lifetime distributions to you and your spouse. Working with a knowledgeable advisor who is trained in this area can't be understated. I work with the best Social Security software and planners in the country: Savvy Social Security Planning for Boomers, found at www.horsesmouth.com.

Do you have an IRA? A 401(k)? A 403(b)? A TSP? Any type of qualified account? Then guess what's coming at age 70 ½??? A very special annual event for you called an RMD—Required Minimum Distribution. Think it's no big deal? If you don't take this RMD (which is taxable) every single year by the required date, you owe the IRS a 50% penalty on the amount you were supposed to take. Will the IRS know if you don't take it? What do you think? ☺

Another issue with IRAs is related to "rollovers." Until recently, most people "thought" they could do as many "60 day rollovers" from an IRA account as they wanted to as long as they put the money back into a qualified IRA account within 60 days. They usually learned the facts the hard way, when they learned from their CPA or the IRS that their account was no longer an IRA and the distribution or rollover was fully taxable.[ii] On January 28th, 2014, the tax court ruled in the Bobrow case that the once-per-year IRA rollover limit applies to *all* of a person's IRAs and not to each IRA separately, as was the case in the past. Effective January 1st, 2015, Traditonal and Roth IRAs are combined for purposes of the once-per-year rule. Checks made directly to a receiving institution for an IRA will qualify as a trustee to trustee transfer. However, if you take possession of the funds and expect to do a "rollover" as you have done in the past, new rules apply. If you do not comply with these rules, you could lose

www.guaranteedsafemoney.com

23

your IRA and it would be fully taxable to you. Has your current advisor made you aware of these rollover regulations and how they affect your ability to move money from your IRAs to new locations? If not, why not?

In this book, I'll share some real-life stories to bring honesty and clarity to help you avoid scams and understand why picking the *right* financial advisor is so important. But before that, I'll share another Ed Slott quote that deals with item # 6 – "The #1 thing that will separate you from the retirement of your dreams is... TAXES!"

Simply put, once you pay a tax, that money is gone—*forever!* If you weren't supposed to pay that tax or could have avoided it, you threw that money away. There is no nice or easy way to say that. I'll discuss this more later in the book, but I want you to know that this is a major area of focus in my financial planning business for my clients.

WORKING WITH THE WRONG FINANCIAL ADVISOR

I was teaching a retirement planning course at Drury University when a husband came up to me during a break, and I will never forget what he said. He gave me permission to share his story but not his identity. To keep things simple, I'll call him Sam and his wife Alice.

"Brad," he said, "I just want to tell you, I'm really enjoying the class." He went on, "I'm not worried about our retirement," he said, "because we are flush." That's the word he used; he said, "We are flush with our retirement accounts."

He was 65 years old, and he said, "I'll probably wait till I'm 70 to retire; but honestly, we don't really need my current income. My wife couldn't come to this class, and I would really like her to sit in on your next class. Sometime after this class (which lasted three weeks) is over, we'll come by and show you where things are, but I'm really not worried about our financial future. We're good, we're flush."

"Sam" came in a few weeks later and introduced me to Alice. They showed me where their retirement funds were, and I got a sick feeling in my stomach right off the bat.

I need to pause here and tell you about my credentials and qualifications when it comes to IRAs. I'm an Ed Slott Master Elite IRA advisor. Ed Slott is America's IRA expert, and he is quoted often in the Wall Street Journal, appearing on CNN, CNBC and Fox News regularly. He has five national best sellers and he has had several financial shows air on PBS over recent years. His shows have raised more money for PBS than any other show in the history of Public Broadcast Television. "Stay Rich for Life" and "Retirement Rescue" are two of his most recent shows which may have aired in your local area. Ed has approximately 360 National Advisors who train under him, and I'm one of those 360. There are Elite Advisors and Master Elite Advisors, and as a Master Elite, I've worked directly under him for four years. So, I feel well qualified to evaluate IRAs.

I noticed the name of an investment company on a return Sam showed me, and I said, "Tell me a little bit about these accounts that you have here." These were IRA accounts, which is my specialty area. I asked, "Can you show me an annual statement so that we can see how these accounts have performed over the last couple of years?"

They said, "Well, that's just it. They haven't been giving us any copies of returns or annual statements the last couple of years," which immediately raised another red flag for me.

I said, "So ... the money's there and you trust ..."

"Oh yeah, yeah, oh yeah, the advisor that we have this invested with, he goes to church with us." They said, "We will say this, his boss doesn't go to church with us, but he does and we trust him. We trust him with our life savings."

I said, "Okay. I'll tell you what. This is what I want you to do the next time you have a meeting. I want you to ask for a detailed printout of the account to see how the money is performing. And ask them this question: "What will the process be for you to move a portion of that money as a direct trustee-to-trustee transfer to another account."

They said, "Okay, we'll ask him that."

Their next meeting was the following week and they called me back pretty quickly and wanted to get back together. "Man, we got them around the table, the gentleman from church who's our advisor and the president of the company, and we asked them about these accounts and they couldn't provide a statement for the account."

Sam and Alice were told, "This is a different kind of statement and a different kind of account, and you have to wait until it comes due this next year on your anniversary date." But, Sam said, "They told us that we were down about $160,000 on those accounts."

How did that happen? For the last four years, the market has been rising. Up, up, up! But these accounts were down significantly, with a loss of $160,000. Sam and Alice were sick! They immediately asked, "Well, if we want to move this money, how will we go about doing it?"

They were met with resistance and their fears were confirmed. They immediately requested to liquidate their IRAs in the most tax-efficient manner, the way I had instructed them to do so. They went into the meeting prepared.

So we've moved all of their accounts, to stop the bleeding. They did lose a total of over $160,000 from their retirement accounts because of their investment choices and the advisors they chose to work with. The money is simply not there, it's gone. To make matters worse, Alice's 90-year-old mother still has a very large sum of money invested there. They'll move that as soon as they can, but they were told it has to stay there until the anniversary date. They have absolutely 0% faith that that money will be there because it's in the same type of account where they lost $160,000.

Sam and Alice came to me because they knew my background. They've met with me probably six times now, but they're still terrified that I may be the same kind of person who lost half their retirement money. They've been burned. They went from being "flush" to, as Alice says, "being absolutely convinced I'm going to have to work for the rest of my life."

I'm doing my best to give them peace of mind, to assure them that they won't have to keep working. Why? Because just as with Bob, I've helped them reposition what they have with contractual guarantees into several different buckets. I've helped them turn on what I call the "faucet"—the income—from one bucket while the others grow with contractually guaranteed income riders so they will never, ever run out of money. I've been working with them for about three months now, and they are slowly recovering from their experience. It's still very, very painful for them, but I hear from them often and it's so nice to hear Alice say, "I am finally getting the *best sleep* I've had in a really long time." This past week, she referred some very close friends to the financial planning course I teach at OTC. With what she has experienced, that says a lot about her peace of mind.

THE YO-YO ECONOMY

This real-life story isn't unique. This type of thing happens to other people, scaring them to death and sometimes wiping them out financially. I'm going to quote Ed Slott now, and I will throughout this book because he's a very credible source. He's

America's IRA expert. He says, "We are in a YO-YO economy." That means, "You're On Your Own."

You have to do your own due diligence. You can't simply trust the name on the door, whether it's Merrill Lynch or Edward Jones or another big name in the investment world. Or a big name in the banking industry. You need to do your own research to know about an advisor, about their background, to find out what kind of training they've received and why they're recommending certain moves or products for you. You need to understand that when they say, "This is what's best for you," they may not really *know* what's best; or, what they really mean is, "This is what's best for me and my firm."

They think they're giving you the right advice, but they're not, and they don't know that they don't know the right direction for you to take with your retirement funds. (Remember what Will Rogers said.) Your advisor may have helped you build your retirement savings and that's great, but once you start taking distributions from your qualified retirement account, everything changes. No one should leave this stage of his or her money management to chance. In most cases, if your advisor doesn't do things correctly and you follow their advice, costly mistakes can be made that cannot be corrected easily. That's why I'm part of the special group of advisors working under Ed Slott.

As one of the 360 national advisors working directly under Ed, I receive ongoing training every year on 401(k)s, IRAs, TSPs and qualified accounts. If a law or an IRS ruling takes place regarding retirement accounts, I know about it almost immediately—within 24 hours—and I wouldn't trade that connection to knowledge about qualified retirement accounts for anything. I want you to be aware that most financial advisors and brokers don't get these updates and are unaware of these pitfalls.

My dad worked for Merrill Lynch for 17 years, and we know what goes on behind the scenes. Investment firms are in business to make money, and they have a limited number of options available to offer you. They don't have the types of products and services I can offer, or they don't make much money on them so you won't hear about them from a broker. Typically, they want to turn the highest profit possible, and that is the motivating factor behind their advice.

You're on your own. You had better find out what is motivating your financial advisor. Is their advice in your best interest? Is it legitimate? Or is it motivated by their own greed or their firm's greed and their desire for advancement?

CHAPTER

5

WHY IS YOUR MONEY IN THE STOCK MARKET?

SHOULD YOU TAKE THE DEAL?

I use the example of the show *Deal or No Deal* when talking to people about where they have their retirement money. You may remember this show, hosted by Howie Mandel, which ran from 2005-2009. Contestants would choose a briefcase and then eliminate remaining briefcases one at a time, hoping to find the big prize in the briefcase they originally chose. After a few briefcases were revealed, the show's banker would make the contestant a cash offer to quit the game. If the contestant refused, the game continued, with the banker periodically making   offers until there were only two briefcases remaining.

At this point, the contestant could trade the original briefcase for the other one left in play, winning whatever was in the briefcase they chose. Out of 273 contestants, only two ever won the big prize of $1,000,000.[iii]

This is something like the way I work with my clients. I give them the options available to them and they say, "Deal," or, "No deal." They can take the option of risk—of potentially losing their money—if they want to, or they can choose the option of guaranteed growth and a lifetime of income that they can never outlive.

Whenever I watched *Deal or No Deal*, there was always a contestant who was offered a good sum of money by the banker to quit the game, and I remember thinking, *"That's probably more money than that person has ever received at any one time in their life. Why not take the sure thing?"* Rational thinking tells you that taking the offer would be a wise choice. Sure, he could possibly win more if he kept playing, but he could also lose, ending up with far less and in some cases nothing. I enjoyed watching the contestants contemplate their choices.

Many times a spouse or a family member would be standing near them, pleading with her to take the offer from the banker, but sure enough, almost every time human nature and greed would eventually win out and the contestant would gleefully shout, "No deal!" Anyone who's watched the show knows all too well how this usually turned out. The contestant would take on too much risk, would end up looking foolish, and would go home with a fraction of what she could have won if she had taken the offer from the banker. Sometimes she went home with almost nothing.

Maybe it's O.K. to risk losing everything on a game show. After all, you start out with nothing. You're only risking "house" money.

But can you take that kind of risk with your retirement and life savings? Right now, you may be looking at your retirement money and trying to decide, *"Deal, or no deal?"* You've worked your entire life to build up your nest egg, and you don't need your retirement to suffer from a bad deal. You can't afford a risky situation, fraught with peril. You don't need to wonder if you'll have to keep working the rest of your life. *You can't afford a bad deal.*

Leaving it to Chance

Most of you were taught at a very young age, perhaps even in college, to get a job and start working toward your retirement. On your first day of work, you probably met with someone from the human resources department and learned all about having a 401(k). They explained about your employer matching your contributions and the advantages of using pretax money from your paycheck to fund your retirement.

What they probably *didn't* tell you when you signed up for that 401(k) plan was that you had just made a deal in a game of chance and that you had entered into a lifelong agreement with Uncle Sam. Most people in their early twenties don't have a clue about taxes. They know nothing about Social Security or required minimum distributions or the effect of deferred taxes and why should those things matter anyway, right?

You're young and you should take some chances to get ahead and reach your goals in life. Right? This isn't always the best advice to follow when it comes to financial planning in a post 9/11 world. As I said before, while *Deal or No Deal* was on TV only two people in the United States ever won the top prize. Now did you hear that? *Two people* actually hit the home run by risking all their earnings and gambling it in a game of chance.

Over the years, I've seen far too many similarities, with far too many people, between the game show *Deal or No Deal* and their real life retirement accounts. The problem is, when it comes to your retirement, this isn't a game. You've worked and saved your entire life, sacrificing income for years to put money back for your retirement—money you could have been using. Instead, you were putting it into your IRA or your 401(k). And it could be gone overnight due to something totally beyond your control, like a 40% drop in the stock market in 2008. Haven't you worked much too hard to leave your future security to chance?

Leaving things to chance is for the young and the rich, or for those who can afford losses because they have the luxury of time. Or for those who, because they have money, think they can afford to lose. If you're like most Americans, those with less than $5,000,000 in retirement assets, losing the game is devastating. When you're at or near retirement, you usually don't have time to recoup your losses from playing the game. I say you *usually* don't have time, because anybody can get lucky. Maybe you lost a lot of money over the last decade but you get a chance to play the game again, and if you're lucky enough, you get back what you lost.

You might feel an incredible sense of relief if you do. Maybe you even feel proud of yourself. But wait a minute. Time out. Why would you be happy to lose something and get it back? Wouldn't it have been better never to lose it in the first place? Wouldn't it have been better to participate in something risky like the market, without any risk of losing it? I mean, hel-*lo!*

WHERE'S THE STOCK MARKET GOING?

On January 25th, 2017, the Stock Market did something it has never done before: it broke the 20,000 point barrier. As a matter of fact, since the election of President Donald Trump on November 8th, 2016, the Dow Jones increased approximately 9.5% in just 42 days. This was the 2nd fastest 1,000 point gain in the history of the stock market. The 3rd fastest 1,000 point gain took 59 days and it occurred in 2007. By the way, do you remember what happened shortly after this in 2008?

I'd like to share an article with you that was written by Christopher Mistal. This appeared in the Stock Trader's Almanac in May of 2014. The Stock Trader's Almanac is considered "the authority on stock market cycles." The editor in chief of the Stock Trader's Almanac is Jeff Hirsch. Jeff makes frequent appearances on CNBC, Fox and Bloomberg. In this article, they talk about bull and bear markets and they revealed the following:

> Using a 20% decline as the definition of a bear market, there have been 11 bull markets, including the current one, and 10 bear markets since 1949. The previous 10 bull markets lasted an average of 1,770 calendar days and produced gains of 161.4%. Within these 11 bull markets, there were 22 corrections, ranging from 10 to 19.9%, for an average of two corrections per bull market. The current bull market, at 1,891 days and 180.5% gain, is above average in duration and magnitude, but average when it comes to the number of corrections.[iv]

Keep in mind this article was written in May of 2014 and following this the market has continued to grow for 3 more years, hitting an all time record high and cresting 20,000 points for the first time in history.

So exactly what does that mean to the average investor?

It simply means this: the bull market from 2009 through early 2014 had been well above average in overall growth, and yet well below average regarding the number of mini corrections that have taken place during that same timeframe. (See below for further explanation of this.) Why does this matter, you may ask? I ask you to listen closely to what the article says next. The article continues,

> The S&P 500's current streak of 955 days without a 10% correction, is nearly twice the average number of days between past corrections. But unlike past streaks of similar or greater strengths, the current streak is most likely the result of unprecedented Fed liquidity, rather than actual economic performance. Based upon past corrections, the current streak could easily last much longer or could just as easily end any day.

In January of 2016, the S&P 500 dropped approximately 5.5%. And the beginning of February 2016 wasn't much better. You probably remember watching the Dow drop from 17,425 to 15,998 in early 2016. The remainder of 2016 continued the up and down trend until the election of Donald Trump on November 8th, 2016. Did the 1,400 point drop in the market in January and early February 2016 take you back to 2008 and make you wonder if the beginning of the next 40% CRASH was coming? Unfortunately, Americans tend to suffer from what I call "financial short-term memory loss" when it comes to the stock market.

It seems to be a "what have you done for me lately" for most people. When the markets are up, as they have been from 2009 to 2017, people tend to forget about 2008 and 2001, when they lost almost 40% of their retirement savings. With the current state of the economy, why do you think the stock market has continued to increase for the past seven years? Does it make sense to you that the stock market will continue to push higher and higher when you hear reports every single day that our economy is in such a terrible mess? Does it confuse you even more that Wall Street wants to paint a rosy picture for you and tells you to buy now, when our nation's debt clock looks like a picture of the Energizer bunny that's about to explode? Can you fathom how much money 20 Trillion dollars is, and the fact that our national debt grows by over 100 million dollars every hour of every single day?

Just to help you understand this a little bit better, let me explain our nation's debt in terms you can understand. According to www.nationaldebtclock.org in January of 2017, our national debt is growing by $27,762.94 per second. The interest on our national debt grows by $14,103 every second! That's $444,760,771,541 in interest a year. This represents $63,110.59 of debt PER PERSON. Do you get it now? It doesn't take a rocket scientist to figure out that the stock market is falsely over-inflated because our government keeps printing money, and as soon as they stop doing that, Pop! Goes the weasel. I'm reminded of another childhood nursery rhyme:

Humpty Dumpty sat on a wall,

Humpty Dumpty had a great fall.

All the king's horses and all the king's men,

Couldn't put Humpty Dumpty together again.

Is your retirement account going to be exactly like this nursery rhyme? Will your retirement and your future income break apart like Humpty Dumpty so that it can't be put back together again?

I always tell my listening audience the truth, and the truth, readers, is this: my listeners continue to call in to my radio program and move millions and millions of dollars out of the stock market and into the lifetime guarantees of Safe Money accounts. Why are they doing this? Because people nearing retirement know it's simply a matter of time before the market takes its next major correction. If you fear the same thing, you need to read on.

A FEW FACTS

I know many people are only convinced by facts and numbers. The people who are pro-stock market will say that over the course of any segment of time in our financial history, the stock market has always provided a higher rate of return than any other investment strategy. And that was true—until we hit 2001.

If you have any investments, you'll notice they always have a disclaimer in their reports saying, "Past performance does not guarantee future returns." I believe the same general principle applies to the market, especially today. We have no evidence or proof that the market is going to come back to the way it was in the '70s, '80s or '90s. We have no proof that it will stay where it is now without taking a major correction or even bottoming out again as it did in 2001. Or 2008. And that can be scary.

Here's a very interesting market fact that I think you will appreciate. One dollar invested in the S&P 500 stock market index on May 31, 1995, in a tax-deferred account would have nearly quadrupled in its value, to $3.95 on a total return basis, by February 28, 2013; or in other words, after seventeen years and nine months. Not bad, for a one dollar investment. Think how much a larger initial sum would be worth.

However, the original dollar doubled in value from $1.00 to $1.94 by January 31, 1998, only two years and eight months after the investment. At that point, things looked great! But then what happened? It took *another* **15 years** for that total to double again to $3.95. Why is that? Because the market is volatile—all those ups and downs and corrections, and the major drops in 2001 and 2008, meant that the one dollar investment was sometimes nearly worthless on its way to being worth $3.95 in 2013.

So I have to ask, which market are you in right now? Are you invested in the market that will double your money every two years and eight months? Or are you invested in the market that will take more than 15 years to double your money? You see, if you are nearing or in retirement and you're taking distributions from your accounts, that is a *very* important question.

If your retirement money is guaranteed to double in two years and eight months, then you don't have anything to worry about, do you? But...if you're taking distributions from your retirement account and it's taking *15 years* for your money to double even before you start taking money from it, then you have a major problem, don't you? You're going to run out of money before you run out of life. You'll be living every retiree's number one fear. But you don't have to live in fear. That's why I love my job: because I help eliminate the number one fear for my clients.

I'll share some more S&P 500^v history to provide some facts that illustrate my point a little further. On May 31, 2013, the S&P 500 had returned 15.37% year-to-date, which was its best January-to-May index performance since 1997, when the S&P gained 15.44% in the first five months of the year. The stock market then went on to gain 33.44% for the rest of 1997. Of course, my job is to relay *all* the facts, not just part of them. If you're feeling really secure right now with stock market investments at your age, then keep your ears open for a minute.

You see, it would be a great story if it ended with that 33.4% gain in 1997, but that's not the end of the story. The rest goes like this: the worst June to December period in stock market history occurred the following year (1998), with a loss of 34.5%. Now, how ironic is that? One of the best gains in stock market history was followed by the worst loss in market history. To top it off, the loss was greater than the gain, ending the two-year period with a 1.1% loss.

Do you ever hear people say, "I just can't seem to get ahead for losing?" Maybe that statement originated from people who have spent their lives investing in risky, volatile markets. When you invest in a stock market or any other volatile account, never be surprised if your account statements resemble a roller coaster ride, going up and down, and up and down... and down again. Some of those down periods are long and steep. Long, steep drops may be a lot of fun on a rollercoaster ride, but it's definitely *not* fun to see them on your IRA, 401(k) or retirement account balance sheet.

WHY I LOVE MY JOB

That's why I love my job, because I can take the number one fear of retirees—that they'll run out of money before they run out of life—completely out of the equation. I can get them off that retirement savings rollercoaster that's been scaring them to death. With the lifetime income benefit on a Safe Money account, my clients have exactly that—a stream of income that is contractually guaranteed to last as long as they live. No pieces to try to fit back together. No lost income to try to recoup. I *love* sitting down with clients for the first time and showing them how this works.

Once they understand it, it's such a blessing to see the expressions on their faces when they realize they'll never have to worry about running out of money ever again. And it's icing on the cake when they realize they'll get to pass on whatever is left in their retirement accounts to their intended beneficiaries.

That's why I've spent my time showing clients how to say goodbye to risk and volatility forever when it comes to their retirement accounts. I show them how to say "Hello!" to peace and security. How? I do this by rolling over their risky stock market accounts from volatile markets to stable Safe Money accounts.

CHAPTER

6

HISTORY DOESN'T REPEAT ITSELF

BUT IT USUALLY RHYMES

Do games like Pong, Ms. Pacman, Adventure, Asteroids, Space Invaders, Frogger, Centipede and Pitfall bring back fond memories to you? All these games came from Atari, and if you were alive during the '70s and '80s there's a good chance this brings back many happy memories. Nearly every American teenager (and many adults) either owned an Atari, wished they owned an Atari, went out of their way to find a friend who owned an Atari or spent quarter upon quarter at the local arcade, trying to get their fill of fun playing Atari games.

The Atari games were pure genius. They broke new ground by introducing Pong, actually starting the age of the video arcade and home video games. No one had ever seen anything more fun and easy to use. It was virtually addictive and enjoyed by practically everyone, including grandma. What began with that simple "tennis" game "Pong" eventually grew into a national phenomenon with over 20 very popular games and millions of loyal followers, similar to Apple's followers today. People lined up and waited for hours, even overnight, to buy the latest Atari game as soon as it was released.

Now, thinking back to those glorious days of yesteryear, remembering all the fun you had with Atari games, let me ask you something; "Is Atari still relevant today?" Don't laugh too hard, because of course, the answer is, "No, not at all." So then, I'd like to ask, "What happened to Atari?"

How's Your Vision?

The answer is very simple. The founders of Atari lost their vision. They changed ownership, and after the video game crash in 1983, the company was never the same. One of the main reasons they slowly became extinct was they stopped investing in new ideas and they stopped creating exciting games for their very loyal customers. This opened the door for Nintendo to come in with games like Super Mario Brothers (which is still popular today). Nintendo quickly became the dominant company in today's video game arena. Sadly, after a short time Atari was old news and became a forgotten name.

Now, you may be thinking, "How is that related to my retirement accounts?" Go back to where I said, "The founders of Atari *lost their vision.*" Does your broker have a vision for you? Or have you been given the same old advice regarding your retirement accounts for the past 10 to 15 years—or longer? When was the last time your broker sat down with you and did an honest, thorough reevaluation of your current retirement plan?

Preparing for Change

Has your broker given you any new creative ideas in the past five years? How about in the past year? Think about it. Our world changes constantly. The financial landscape is constantly evolving, and right now it's changing dramatically. Tax laws, retirement account limitations and healthcare have all changed significantly in recent years. All these things will affect your retirement planning and your future distributions from your qualified retirement accounts. Has your broker's advice changed along with all these changes—or do you continue to hear the same thing?

Are you still hearing, "Don't worry about it—put it in the stock market and let it ride. If there's a loss, it will come back because the markets always come back."

That may have worked in the past, but we live in a completely different world now. If you're still getting that kind of advice, it's time for you to make significant changes to your retirement planning. If you don't, you will find yourself in the same boat as Atari—out of date, irrelevant and bankrupt.

I've served hundreds of local clients over the past decade, and I specialize in guaranteed Safe Money accounts with contractual guarantees, which provide all the clients using them with lifetime income for them and their spouses. By taking the time to listen to your needs and goals, as I do for all of my clients, I can let *your* dreams dictate the type of account we set up for you. You probably don't realize this, but the purpose of money should dictate its position. I can't know where to invest your money until you tell me what you want it to do for you.

You'll Need a Boat

No matter what your personal beliefs are, it's a matter of historical evidence that our earth once endured a great flood. I believe that right before that flood a man named Noah had the vision to listen to the information he was given, to follow the instructions he was given and to build a giant boat—"Noah's Ark."

He built this boat before a drop of rain ever fell to earth. It made no sense to the people around him. They thought he was crazy for building this huge boat. Why would anyone play it so safe when there was no sign of danger ahead? Then the rain came and the waters rose. Tragedy struck, and they all wished they'd made similar plans. Their failure to plan, to prepare for the flood Noah foretold, cost them everything they had, including their lives.

Right now, the stock market looks good. It's gone up, up, up for many years, and to many people "playing it safe" seems foolish. Who in their right mind would prepare for the future by playing it safe when things are going so well and the markets are up? Why not take the risk?

Maybe we should look at recent history to be reminded of the vicious market cycles. Do you remember the losses you and millions of others experienced in 2001 and in 2008? Many people are just now getting back to where they were in their retirement accounts six years ago. Could 2017 be the next cycle where the market takes a major hiccup? What are you doing today to protect your most important assets before the unthinkable happens? Because, it will happen. Something in the future will rock your financial world. Whether it's something personal, like death or divorce, or a national or world event like a stock market crash or a September 11-type terrorist attack. *Something* will rock your world. History has proven this repeatedly.

It may not be an isolated event that rocks your financial world. It could be something that's creeping up on us right now. For a quick dose of reality, open your computer and go to our nation's debt calculator. That's www.USdebtclock.org. As I look at this website, I realize that our nation's debt is now $17 trillion. Not billion, that's trillion with a "T," and our *real* U.S. debt total is more than *$70 trillion*. That's a figure you never hear anyone talking about, the "real U.S. total debt."

You've never heard about this? Most people haven't, and I would encourage you to do some research on this as it does affect you and your financial future. You can go to the following sites for more information:

- http://www.thenewamerican.com/usnews/congress/item/16264-university-of-california-study-the-national-debt-is-really-70-trillion

- http://www.dailymail.co.uk/news/article-2380987/Leading-economist-says-US-national-debt-actually-86-8TRILLION.html

At a very high level, this total debt figure includes housing guarantees, FDIC guarantees, Social Security and Medicare guarantees and other government trust fund liabilities.

I could discuss the many different aspects of how these two things alone could greatly affect your retirement, but that would require multiple chapters and a new book. My point is simply this: we will reap what we've been sowing in this country, and whether or not you're prepared for that is up to you.

I spend time with my clients, helping to protect their life savings by preparing for what is to come. I'll make that same offer to you—to listen to you, to understand your needs and

50   www.guaranteedsafemoney.com

goals, to prepare you for the future and to protect your savings—that I've made to hundreds of other clients who have received the benefit of this planning.

7

INCOME, NOT IF-COME

GET OFF THE ROLLERCOASTER

Like many people I know, you've probably ridden your fair share of rollercoasters in your lifetime. We're blessed here in Ozark to live close to Silver Dollar City, where they recently introduced a new rollercoaster ride. For months that ride's line was the longest in the park. No one, no matter their age, could wait to get on that ride and enjoy the thrills of the ups and downs and twists and turns of a good rollercoaster. For a thrill-seeker, there's nothing quite like the feeling in the pit of your stomach when you take that first gigantic drop to the bottom of the track. The bigger the better.

Now, isn't that ironic? The faster and steeper a rollercoaster is, the better we like it, the more fun we have. But if I describe your retirement account using rollercoaster words, you're not happy at all. If, when speaking of your retirement account, I mention that feeling in the pit of your stomach caused by the first major drop to the bottom, or the ups and downs and twists and turns, it gives you flashbacks to 2001 and 2008 when your retirement account dropped as much as 40%. That's not the type of thrill you're seeking, is it?

Aren't we interesting creatures? The very same people who love the ups and downs and the twists and turns in amusement park rides hate the ups and downs in their retirement accounts. Well, we all love part of that ride, don't we? We love the *ups*, we just don't like the downs and the twists and the turns. But what if you could get on a retirement rollercoaster that took you higher and higher, showing you amazing views at the top, without ever taking you through a downward spiral? Wouldn't that be great? Sometimes we get caught up in the fever of a bull market, thinking it's like a rollercoaster that always keeps going *up*. But that's impossible, isn't it? It absolutely can't happen.

The market did keep going up, from 2002 to 2007 and from 2009 to 2017; but then, right about the time you've forgotten you're on a rollercoaster, you reach the top and... Whoops! What happens next? That's right, things like 9/11 happen. Things like 2001, or economic downturns as we saw in 2008 or things like January of 2014 happen. In January 2014, the longest bull market in history came to a screeching halt when the Dow dropped from 16,500 to 15,600 in only two weeks, closing the month down almost 6%. It recovered briefly, but then it dropped over 600 points again in early August of 2014, taking the year-to-date total of the S&P to -0.5%.

I remember the first two days when the market started dropping in January of 2014. I received a call on a Friday afternoon from a potential client who had been listening to my radio program, and he simply said, "Brad, the market is starting to do what you've been talking about and I've lost $10,000 in the past two days." There's that feeling in the pit of your stomach that no one wants to have. Then in early August 2014, the market dropped over 600 points in just four days, costing retirees thousands and thousands and thousands of dollars.

After this, we experienced January and February of 2016. In January of 2016, the S&P 500 dropped approximately 5.5%. And then it continued to drop in February of 2016. You probably remember watching the Dow drop from 17,425 at the end of 2015 to 15,998 in early 2016. Do you remember how you feel every time this happens and you have money invested in accounts that are not protected against loss?

Friends, if you're in retirement or you're nearing retirement and you remember what 2001 and 2008 felt like, then keep reading. Current academic research says that 60% of all retirees will fail in retirement and have to go back to work—that's three out of five seniors. Something is clearly not working with the one-size-fits-all mentality for financial planning that goes like this, "Give your broker your money, pay him to invest it and manage it in the stock market, and let it ride." Friends, that model no longer works in today's world because over time history has shown that the S&P 500, which was the best way to invest in the long run, was a pre-9/11 model that has not proven to be successful since then.

Do the Math

Recovering from a Loss

I help clients stop losses and fees while learning how to compete with inflation and lowering their taxes. When you do that, you'll come out way ahead in the end. I like to ask radio listeners and retirement planning class students this question; "If you invest $100,000 in the stock market and it drops by 50%, how much money will you have left?" They always get the answer right—it's $50,000 minus, of course, the fees you paid to your advisor for investing it. Then I ask the following question, "How much would the market have to gain back, for you to get even?"

This is where it gets interesting. Most people will immediately answer 50% and follow the answer with obvious logic. If I lose 50%, then it will take a 50% gain to get back to even. However, the correct answer is, "It depends." It will take at least a 100% gain to get back to even. When I say this, I get a deer in the headlights look back from my students. They're in shocked disbelief.

You don't believe me? Do the math. Take $100,000 and multiply it by a 50% loss and the answer is $50,000. Then take $50,000 and multiply it by 50% gain, and the answer is $25,000. Add $25,000 to your existing $50,000 balance and you reach your new total: $75,000. *Not* your original $100,000.

You see, losses hurt. It takes a 100% gain to correct a 50% loss. Depending on how long that recovery takes, you also have to recover from advisory fees and inflation, so you may need as much as a 120% recovery. So what it will take to recover from your 50% loss varies. *But it will always be* at least 100%.

GUARANTEEING YOUR INCOME

The other one-size-fits-all retirement strategy is the famous 4% Withdrawal Rule, and it isn't working either. This rule suggests that once you retire, you should be able to withdraw 4% of your retirement savings in the first year, adjust that percentage for inflation each year thereafter, and safely live off the income for 30 years. The decade of 2001 to 2010 proved to millions of retirees that this didn't work if your money was invested in the stock market or any other form of risk-based account. Do you remember Bob's situation from the introduction to this book?

The problem with the 4% Withdrawal Rule is that most financial advisors never give their clients an illustration that includes the possibility of a significant correction, much less a lengthy bear market, when they're discussing that rule with them. They never bring up the retirees who, like Bob, didn't anticipate the losses of 2008, or those before him who retired right before 9/11. They simply rattle off the 4% Withdrawal Rule and leave clients to assume that it will work. With no caveats. Or guarantees. There are no back-up plans for what happens when the market drops 40% while the owners are taking distributions from their accounts.

Clients need guarantees in retirement. That's what you need and what you should demand. You need the safety and security of knowing that your income will last as long as you do. Today, many retirement plans end up looking like spring thunderstorms. Everything's calm one minute and then, boom! Ominous dark clouds arise the next. When those clouds roll in, you have no protection from the wind, rain and hail they bring—you simply have to hang on and hope to endure the storm. If you endure, you look around, assess the damage, and hope and pray that your retirement boat is still floating. Then you determine how well you're able to navigate the waters ahead with what you have left.

What I do for my clients is completely different. Picture a beautiful calm spring day and imagine yourself sitting on the edge of a big serene lake. As you sit there, enjoying the trees and the flowers, along comes a flock of swans, gracefully swimming in the water. There are very few images this powerful, and that's what I help my clients achieve—a peaceful retirement. I use the acronym SWAN to symbolize "sleeping well at night." All my clients do exactly that; they sleep well at night knowing that not one single penny of their retirement savings is at risk from the storms of life that lie ahead.

No matter what happens in the future, 100% of their principal is protected from the storms. You can't place a value on the comfort that provides to your family, if your plans for the future ensure that you will never run out of money before you run out of life.

In his book "Money – Master the Game: 7 Steps to Financial Freedom, Tony Robbins says: "I often ask people 'What are you investing for?' The responses are wide and diverse: Returns, Growth, Assets, Freedom, Fun. Rarely do I hear the answer that matters most: INCOME!!!!! We all need an income that we can count on." (Pg 406-407)

He goes on to talk about "income insurance" and what that is. He describes income insurance as "a guaranteed way to know for certain that you will have a paycheck for life without having to work for it in the future – to be absolutely certain that you will never run out of money." (Pg 407) Then he goes on to describe "the only financial vehicle on the planet" that gives you guaranteed lifetime income with no risk, no fees, and 100% principal protection. Are you curious to know what type of account it is? It is called a Fixed Indexed Annuity.

Tom Hegna, author of Amazon best-selling book "Paychecks and Playchecks" suggests that only 19% of people in retirement have a guaranteed lifetime pension. Federal government retirees account for the bulk of these lucky retirees, representing 16% of all the people with guaranteed lifetime pensions. Those numbers are staggering. Only 3% of all retirees, outside of government employees, currently have a guaranteed lifetime pension. (And I'm not talking about Social Security.) I have to ask, "Which group do you fall into? Are you in the other 81% of the population, searching for a guaranteed form of retirement income that will last the rest of your life?"

Avoiding the Consequences of a Bear Market

What are you doing to establish a guaranteed lifetime income for you and your family? As the first month of 2014 ended, the stock market started getting particularly bumpy, with the Dow dropping from 16,500 to 15,600 in only 10 days. It looked like it could have been the beginning of the end to the longest bull market in history. In February 2014, I was in Denver, Colorado, at a national producer's conference, receiving an award along with five other financial advisors. On my last morning there, February 1, I picked up a copy of *USA Today*, and was struck by what I saw on the front page.

In bold letters it said, "Down January for stocks is bad omen for 2014.[vi]" The article, by Adam Shell, suggests that, historically, the stock market performance in January sets the tone for the rest of the year. Since January of 2014 ended nearly 4% down, that didn't bode well for the rest of 2014. Shell goes on to say, "Big January losses in 2000 and in 2008 set in motion the two recent bear markets, or drops of 20% or more. That's why the weak start to 2014 is ramping up the fear factor." [vii] He goes on to say,

> The stock downdraft has been driven by a variety of factors colliding at the same time. Financial turmoil in emerging markets such as Turkey and South Africa is the major source of angst, as it has raised concerns about financial contagion. Adding to the anxiety: the Federal Reserve's move to keep "tapering" its market-friendly stimulus and signs of a slowdown in China, the globe's chief growth driver in recent years.

> After last year's 30% gain, the U.S. market is no longer cheap, which makes it more vulnerable to unexpected shocks. [viii]

And finally, "The U.S. stock market, he adds, has gone 850 days without a correction of 10% or more, vs. a correction every 230 days, on average. As a result, the market was overdue for a pullback following last year's big gains." [ix]

In the same article, the chief investment strategist at Moneta Group warns of two risks that could harm the market in 2014, "emerging-market weakness becoming a 1998-99 type of contagion event and spreading to Europe; or a monetary policy mistake, maybe someone raising rates too soon or (being) too aggressive on tapering." [x]

January and February of 2014 looked a lot like January and February of 2016. The Dow Jones and S&P 500 took 4-5%

losses to begin those years and feelings about the market were very cautious and unstable. It started to bring back memories of 2008. The remainder of those years looked a lot like a rollercoaster. It was filled with big up and down swings. Only after the election of President Donald Trump in November of 2016 did the market recover from the inconsistent up and down cycle, ending the year on a high note and pushing the markets to all-time record highs.

If you paid any attention to all the ups and downs of the market during this time period, you probably realized this: We live in one of the most vulnerable financial times we've ever seen. A 2008-type stock market collapse could happen at any minute. No one predicted the collapse of 2008. Your broker didn't foresee it, or you would have been advised to sell everything before you lost 40% of your retirement account. In early 2017, the stock market reached its highest point in history. What advice are you getting from those who are helping you with your retirement account? Is it to "let it ride?" Are you being told, "It's okay, the market will continue to go up and up and up?"

Maybe it will, maybe it won't. Maybe, with the market at all-time highs, we are merely one catastrophic event away from a totally different market. Don't forget what happened in June of 2016 when the now famous "Brexit" news hit the scene. The Dow Jones dropped almost 900 points in two days, making it the biggest two-day drop since August of 2015. And how could possible forget about our nation's current debt? At present, we are just a few thousand dollars away from cresting the 20

Trillion Dollar mark. Try to let that sink in for a few minutes. If you are uncertain about the future of the market, and if you are depending on your current retirement accounts for your future income, why wouldn't you add 10% to your retirement account right now by getting out of a risky market and by rolling it over into a Safe Money account? Then you will never have to worry about the ups and downs of the market again.

The facts are simple—markets go up and markets go down. I don't know what they're going to do next, and neither does your broker, but I do know this—safety in retirement matters. When the markets do drop again, people who have their retirement money protected against loss inside a Safe Money account will not have their income affected. It will not turn into "if-come" overnight. Owners of a Safe Money account have lifetime income guarantees that pay them a monthly pension no matter how long they live. They never have to worry about running out of money before they run out of life.

CHAPTER

8

TAX-FREE BEATS TAXABLE—EVERY TIME

Over the years, I've been blessed to meet many wonderful people and hear the stories of their lives. It's impossible for me to help manage a person's entire life savings without learning the details of their lives. I've met spouses, children, grandchildren and family friends. I recently expanded my business from three offices to six simply to provide room for better interaction with my clients and their families. We host several different client events throughout the year in an effort to stay better connected and to help clients meet other people their age, in the same stages of life.

My clients have made some great friendships with each other by attending these events. But I also hear stories throughout the year that leave me very humbled and even sad. No matter how much I teach—through public training seminars, college retirement classes and on the radio—about preparing for life in retirement, there will always be people who don't take the necessary steps, who end up experiencing life in a way I find tragic. The following true story is shared with permission, although I won't share the names to protect the identity of those involved.

PLANNING FOR DEATH

In the spring of 2014, I received a phone call from a woman in her early 50s. She had listened to my radio program and was desperate for more information. You see, her husband of more than 30 years had been diagnosed recently with terminal cancer and was expected to live only a few more months. This resulted in immediate desperation for her. She'd always been a homemaker and had never worked for a paycheck so she would have no Social Security from her own earnings. Out of necessity and with no education beyond high school, she had just taken a job paying $8 an hour.

When she called, asking to meet with me that day, I cleared my schedule to make room for her. She was devastated. She loved her husband deeply, and her life plan had included nothing except being his spouse and sharing a life together. Now, her husband was dying unexpectedly and very quickly at the age of 63. To learn more about their financial situation and to determine exactly how I could help them, we called her husband to talk to him on speakerphone; he was too weak to make the trip to my office. On that call, I discovered exactly how desperate her situation was.

What I learned was truly heartbreaking. One of my first questions, after learning they had no retirement accounts was, "Do you have life insurance?" You see, no matter how much people think they don't like or don't need life insurance, that thinking always changes when death is imminent. I've never had a single person say, "I sure wish my husband had less life insurance in force when he died. We sure wasted a lot of money on premiums." That simply has never happened. The number one question I *am* asked when a family member dies is, "How much life insurance did they have in force?"

Her husband's answer to the question originally made her feel good, but I knew there was a major problem. He had taken out a $100,000 term life insurance policy only a few years before, which was good news. He would have a great return on that investment. She would definitely receive $100,000 of tax-free money upon his death.

I recognized the bad news immediately, though. They had recently purchased a new home and their mortgage balance was $120,000. In short, she would be left without his income from Social Security, no job experience, no retirement accounts to draw from, a $120,000 mortgage and a total of $100,000 to her name. And it would take at least 30 days to receive that payment from the life insurance company. In case you don't know, at age 52 she is not eligible to receive reduced survivor benefits from Social Security until she reaches age 60. That is eight years of a loss of income. I can assure you that wasn't in their financial plan, but it is the reality she now faces. I teach this to my clients and students in my classes often: failing to plan properly is planning to fail!

Their financial plan, when I first talked to them, was to have her take the $100,000 from the life insurance policy and pay down the house mortgage, leaving only $20,000 on the mortgage. It makes sense, right? Everyone recommends lowering your debts as much as possible. But what about her current and continuing house payment of about $800 a month? Sure, it could be refinanced if she paid it down, but she would *still* have a house payment. Can you make that on an $8 an hour job? What about food, gas, utilities, insurance and emergencies? Health insurance for an individual her age? Medical bills? *You* know how many things there are to pay for on a monthly basis. You know what it takes to survive.

Saying they were in a dire situation is an understatement. To make a really long and painful story short, very few options could help in this situation. You can't create something from nothing. I did help them rethink their plan. I showed them how to best use the $100,000 tax-free payment from the life

TAX-FREE BEATS TAXABLE—EVERY TIME

insurance policy to allow her to stay in her home and pay her monthly bills. Sadly, her husband died much earlier than expected, just four weeks after we first met. She soon learned some harsh lessons about life.

He died on July 31, 2014. What did the Social Security Administration do? They took back his Social Security payment for the month of July. That's right, my friends, if you've not experienced this, your survivors don't get to keep your Social Security payment for the month in which you pass away. Even if you die on the last day of the month. They take back the entire payment. The deposit that was made into their account in July was taken back and she began scrambling to get the $100,000 death benefit as soon as possible. She was barely able to make ends meet.

Now here's a question for you. "That $100,000 life insurance cost them very little each month, less than $100. How much did it cost them *not* to have more life insurance in force?"

The answer is that it cost them their time, their security, their peace of mind—the list is very, very long. That lack of life insurance protection means she is now forced to work the rest of her life. Retirement is not a possibility; it's not in the game plan. She'll struggle to make ends meet for the rest of her life. For pennies on the dollar, her husband could have had a $500,000 life insurance police in force. How much of a difference would that have made? Would the extra $150 a month in life insurance premiums have changed her life and her financial future? The answer is yes. What other investment, for $150 a month, would have provided a tax-free windfall of $500,000 a mere two years later? Nothing.

Nothing. The stock market won't make that kind of return, bonds won't make that kind of a return, mutual funds won't make that kind of a return, nothing will make that kind of return except for life insurance. America's IRA expert Ed Slott says, "Life insurance is the only legal way to print money." For pennies on the dollar, you return dollars on pennies—tax-free. It's just that simple. What is the most important step you can take today to provide your family, with safety and security, both now and in the future? You can increase your life insurance coverage.

Why do I bring that up? Because when it comes to life insurance, it has been estimated that 95% of all families are under-insured. They simply don't think about what would happen if the primary breadwinner died and they lost that income and all the other benefits he or she provides for the family. Or, if they think about it, they fail to plan for it—to consider all the consequences and ramifications. It's critical to include considerations of the death of a spouse in your retirement planning.

PLANNING STAGES AND GOALS

There are three main stages of retirement planning:

1. Accumulation,

2. Preservation and

3. Distribution.

In the early stages of your life, you are accumulating money and putting it away into your financial accounts: IRAs, Roth IRAs, 401(k)s, life insurance, etc. Hopefully, as you read early in the book, you started this very early in life. The sooner you begin, the better off you will be when you retire.

Then you enter the preservation stage of life. This shift in focus normally comes around age 50 when you realize you can't afford to *lose* money anymore. If you go through a 2001 or a 2008 in your retirement accounts after the age of 50 and take losses of up to 40% in your accounts, your plan to retire at age 65 will be extended for 10-15 years. Simply put, losses hurt. This is when a person should shift their focus from *gaining* to *maintaining* what they have worked so hard to earn. At this point in life, it is no longer the return *on* your money that is the focus, but rather the return *of* your money that matters. Don't go backwards!

Finally, once you hit retirement you start the distribution phase of life. At this point, preservation is still vitally important. Once you begin taking distributions from your retirement accounts, you can't afford to experiences losses and distributions at the same time. I hear about too many people who suffer from what I call the "Triple Whammy" in retirement: Distributions, Losses, and Fees. The combination of those three things in retirement will send you back to work quicker than anything else. *That* is why 60% of current retirement plans fail in this country. I am trying to help people, with proper planning, to protect themselves from ever experiencing that.

You have to know what stage you're in and then communicate your goals and purposes very clearly to your advisor. Then, together, you can plan accordingly. There are four main purposes associated with these stages of retirement and, at each stage, you can only have one main purpose driving you or you risk becoming sidetracked. These four main goals include:

1. Growing your assets,
2. Preserving your assets,
3. Maintaining liquidity and
4. Drawing income.

Too many people try to accomplish too many things at once and get lost in the forest due to the many trees. There are some important things to keep in mind as you're designing your retirement plan. I'll talk about each of these goals in the following pages.

There are two things to think about when your goal is to grow your assets: when to start and where to put your money. First, the mathematical proof of the wisdom of starting early is staggering. Albert Einstein is credited with saying, "The greatest invention of all time is compounded interest." A great example of this can be found in a book I refer to later in this chapter by Patrick Kelly called "Tax-Free Retirement." In Chapter 4 on pages 34-35 he lists a chart that shows the difference between the retirement accounts of Jill and Mark, who start their accounts at different ages. The results are mind-blowing.

Jill started her account at age 19 and contributed $2,000 a year *for 8 years* with an assumed interest rate of 10%. Mark, however, waited to start his contributions until age 27. In other words, he started his contributions the year after Jill stopped hers, and yet he continued the same amount of contributions ($2,000 per year) *for the next 39 years* with the same assumed interest rate of 10%. If you're good at math, you will realize that Mark started his savings plan only 8 years after Jill and he contributed $62,000 *more* than Jill. So who do you think will have *more* money at age 65?

Surely you can guess the answer since I have spent so much time talking about the power of starting early and the power of compounded interest. With those assumed rates, at age 65 Jill would have $1,035,160 and Mark would have $883,185. And she stopped contributing after 8 years! Just think where she would be if she had continued to contribute!

Now imagine that interest compounding inside an account that is 100% protected from losses, fees and taxation. Your fastest track to retiring wealthy begins with Roth IRA's and permanent life insurance. You should own as much of both as you can possibly afford. I'm going to explain, but let me tell you first that I personally have two Roth IRAs and eight life insurance policies.

Protecting Your Assets from Taxes

I touched on it in the previous paragraph about growing assets, but when your goal is preserving your assets, avoiding taxes is extremely important. And there's some disagreement about the method I recommend for avoiding taxes.

In one of his books, a very well known, national bestselling author says that cash value life insurance is one of the worst financial products available. Simply put, that is one of the most inaccurate and terrible pieces of financial advice you'll ever be given. Again, I personally own eight life insurance policies and the tax-free benefit of those policies will provide guaranteed retirement income *and* provide my family with millions of dollars of tax-free income when I'm gone. Without exceptions, no questions asked. No other investment vehicle can make that boast. Again, as I quoted Ed Slott earlier, "Life insurance is the only way to legally print money."

Let me briefly explain. I could take the exact same amount of money I'm investing in my life insurance policies right now and put them into almost any other financial vehicle—gold, silver, other precious metals, real estate, stocks, bonds or mutual funds. Any of today's standard investment modes. Now let's say, for this example, that I'm three years into the savings plan, which is diversified into eight different accounts, when the unthinkable happens—I die unexpectedly. What happens to the taxable value of those diversified accounts? What would be the net gain or loss? The answer is... it depends.

It depends on how risky your investment was and how it performed. Did the stock market move up or down—*overall*—during that three-year period? That would determine whether I had a gain or loss. How much would my heirs owe in taxes on those potential gains? Here's the catch-22. If I made a lot of money during that period (which is certainly my goal), my heirs would owe taxes on all the gains. But if I lost money (which no one wants to do) they would avoid taxes—but their inheritance would be less.

Let's take that same example, though, and invest the same amount of money into eight separate life insurance policies. Some term, some permanent, all for different purposes, but all with the same overall goal in mind. When combined, these policies will provide several million dollars in tax-free death benefits to me and my heirs. You see, I want tax-free income for my retirement and I want tax-free income for my heirs. Tax free beats taxable *every* time! And what happens if I die suddenly three years into that investment plan? The answer is guaranteed tax-free payments to my heirs. They will inherit millions of dollars tax-free. Most people know and understand that.

However, I'll talk now about "where the rubber meets the road." For those people who think life insurance is a terrible investment, what happens if I live after all? Most people think that life insurance is simply for the death benefit. My retirement plans are for living, not for dying. If I live, the answer is, "It's even better."

One hundred percent of the funds I pull out of a life insurance policy, when it's the right kind of policy, are tax-free and they will not affect the taxation of my Social Security benefits. This is where I'm able to meet the important goal of *liquidity*. If my kids need a car and I want to pull funds from my life insurance to buy it for them, the answer is, "Yes. The distribution from my life insurance policy will be tax-free." If I want to buy a home, "Yes, I can make a tax-free withdrawal from my life insurance policy." If I want to take a vacation, I can pay for it using my life insurance, tax-free. I can use it for my kids' or grandkids' college tuition sometime in the future, and it's a tax-free distribution. I can use it for long-term care or nursing home expenses, tax-free. If I want to use money from my life insurance policies instead of borrowing money from my bank, it's tax-free.

This single concept alone, this one capability, is worth the cost of owning the right kind of life insurance policy. I could write an entire book on this subject, but I don't have to. Thankfully, my friend Patrick Kelly has already written two. Be sure to read *Tax Free Retirement* and *The Retirement Miracle*.

When you finish those books, pick up a copy of *The Better Money Method* by Terry Laxton. After reading those books and learning the concepts involving two key IRS codes that allow you to invest in these types of life insurance accounts, you'll know more than 99% of all current financial advisors when it comes to life insurance and what it can do for your family.

Now here are some more questions for you to consider:

1. Can your current investments do that for you?

2. Can you take tax-free distributions from stocks, bonds and mutual funds?

3. Are those accounts, your stocks, bonds and mutual funds, 100% protected from losses and fees?

4. Are the gains on those accounts tax-free?

5. If not, then how much are these investments costing you and your family in the long run?

INSURANCE YOU CAN'T AFFORD TO LIVE WITHOUT

I find it interesting that a famous author and radio personality, who is not a financial advisor and does not have any credentials, licenses, or degrees pertaining to insurance or financial planning, claims that cash value life insurance is one of the worst financial products available. He also says this one page later in the very same book, "Some insurance you can't afford to live without." Wow.

Now, I've read the book and I believe it's an instance of losing sight of the forest for all the trees. I'll ask a few simple questions here to help prove my point.

1. Do you own and pay for home owner's insurance on your home?

The answer is, "Yes," of course.

2. Do you own and pay for car insurance on your car?

Again, the answer is, "Yes," of course. My next question is:

3. Why?

The answer is obvious. If you were to lose your house to a fire or a storm, like a hurricane or a tornado, you would want a 100% guarantee that you're protected against those losses because your home is one of your biggest investments. The answer is the same for your car. What if someone hits you and you lose your car or, God forbid, you couldn't work because of that accident? You want to be protected—you want a 100% guarantee.

And here's my final question (light bulb coming on yet?):

4. Why in the world wouldn't you want to ensure a tax-free retirement?

You work your entire life to save money. You put it into IRAs, 401(k)s, TSPs, CDs, cash accounts and other types of retirement accounts. Literally millions of people risk their life savings in those accounts with zero protection against loss and zero protection against taxation *every single day*. They work their whole lives only to see 40% to 50% disappear overnight.

Do you remember 2001 and 2008? The author who doesn't like life insurance is right about one thing. There *are* some forms of insurance you can't afford to live without. But life insurance is one of those forms. Because life insurance, permanent life insurance and cash value life insurance, gives you 100% guaranteed tax-free protection for your retirement accounts. You simply cannot afford *not* to have it.

78   www.guaranteedsafemoney.com

HATE THOSE ANNUITIES?

Finally, when it comes to the goal of *income*, I'd like to quote Ed Slott, again. He says, "Life insurance doesn't cost, it pays." People who call in to my radio program often ask what type of investment I'm talking about when I mention the Safe Money account and then they will say, "I sure hope it's not an annuity or life insurance. I don't like annuities." I hear this a lot and it always brings up a great question, so I ask them, "So you don't like annuities, really? Now are you sure about that? Let me ask you a question, just to make sure. Are you going to accept your Social Security payments in the future?" What do you think they say?

"Of course," they answer.

Then I'll ask, "Do you have a guaranteed retirement pension from work? If you do, do you plan on taking that payment?" and they always say, "Of course."

Then I'll ask, "Do you have any other form of pension, from the government or anything else, and if so, do you plan on taking that pension payment every month?" The answer is always "Yes."

They want their Social Security; they want their guaranteed pension and—guess what? Every single one of those pensions is an annuity payment. Bottom line, that's what they are.

So why do people say they don't like annuities? Why do they say they don't like life insurance? It's because there is so much bad information and there are so many bad opinions about them floating around. Most people base their opinions on what they've read or what they've heard some brokers say, and it's usually not true. Here's a fact: certain types of annuities are great for a portion of your portfolio. Annuities offer guaranteed pension payments for life. I don't know anyone who wants to call Social Security and say, "Hey, I don't like those checks you keep sending me every month. It really bothers me that these are guaranteed for the rest of my life, so please stop sending the checks." Social Security checks are simply guaranteed annuity payments.

The article "Rethinking the 'buy term and invest the difference' strategy" by Jeff Reed, which was posted on producersweb.com on March 27, 2014, goes into great detail about the importance of buying permanent insurance instead of term insurance. Another great article is called "Buy term and invest the rest—not anymore!" written by Nicholas Paleveda, MBA on April 27, 2013. He talks about the three myths that are associated with the "buy term and invest the rest" philosophy, and then explains why this philosophy is no longer valid. There are many reasons why you should take the time to read this article on producersweb.com.

One final article that's worth your time is "Don't listen to Suze Orman's 'buy term and invest the difference'," posted on producersweb.com on June 24, 2013, by Jeffrey Berson. In this article he says,

To most of us who understand the insurance world and the real choices available for your clients, the advice that Suze Orman gives is, at best, irritating; and at worst, negligent. It is virtually impossible for one piece of advice to be the answer for millions of people all at the same time.

In our world of financial decisions, each client is like a snowflake. No two are alike and no set of circumstances is the same. In Suze's world, everyone is the same and should simply do whatever she says— black or white, no gray.[xi]

If none of the information in this chapter has captured your attention, perhaps this will. When it comes to the thought of something happening to you and leaving your loved ones with a need for income replacement if you weren't here to keep working or if you were unable to work, very few people think about what it would take to replace that income. And very few people think about providing that in a tax-free manner. Remember, if your current plan involves that replacement income coming from an IRA or 401(k) that will be 100% taxable to your heirs, which means they will have *less* money to live on after they pay the taxes due from those distributions.

Many people, financial advisors included, think IRA stands for "Individual Retirement Account." That's not correct! Don't believe me? Go to the irs.gov website and type in "ira" to find the definition for an IRA—it's actually "Individual Retirement

Arrangement." You see, when you have a 401k or an IRA, you have an "arrangement" or an "agreement" with the IRS. They agree to let you defer those taxes, until you take distributions or until you reach age 70 ½, at which point distributions are *required*. You will always pay taxes on those distributions and so will your heirs or any other beneficiary who touches that money!

Now do you realize just how firmly your retirement accounts are connected to the IRS? And if you're like many people, your IRA represents 75-100% of your retirement plan. Are you comfortable with this? Or would you like a different plan that doesn't expose you to so much taxation?

If you currently earn $50,000 per year, it would take $1,000,000 earning 5% to provide the income your family needs to survive once you are gone or disabled. But what if your current investments are only making 1%, like a CD or current interest bearing account? You would need $5,000,000 in assets to replace that income. And that is for someone earning $50,000 annually. What if you make $100,000? $200,000? And this amount doesn't include the money required to pay taxes on distributions from tax-deferred accounts. Perhaps now you can see why it is estimated that 95% of all people are currently underinsured. Don't let this happen to you!

There are so many factors to consider here. If your spouse is under the age of 60, they cannot receive survivor benefits from your Social Security when you die, which would be another major loss of income. If you don't have a pension that passes on to your spouse, this would be another major loss of income. In instances like these, life insurance becomes even more important.

Best-selling author Tom Hegna says, "Death is a permanent problem that we all have to face. It should be solved with permanent life insurance."

I highly recommend reading Ed Slott's book "Stay Rich for Life—Growing and Protecting Your Money in Turbulent Times." In Chapter 12, he discusses in great detail how to select the right life insurance policy and the right agent for you and explains how this will benefit your overall financial plan and estate.

I'm sure you have noticed this regarding just about anything in life, but "educated people" will often have opposing views on the exact same topic. Don't believe me? You can Google or Youtube "life insurance as an investment" and "fixed indexed annuities" and you will find all kinds of negative information about this. Yet, have you ever heard of Tony Robbins? Have you read his 2014 book titled "Money – Master the Game – 7 Steps to Financial Freedom?" In this book he shares the "secrets from the world's greatest financial minds." Would you be surprised to know there are entire sections in this book about the Risks of the Stock Market, the power of Fixed Indexed annuities (which I discussed earlier in this book) and the power of owning Life Insurance as a key part of your income plan (which I discussed in detail in this chapter)?

As a matter of fact, Tony Robbins has two entire sections in his book titled "Upside Without the Downside: Creating a Lifetime Income Plan" (which is about Fixed Indexed Annuities with Income Riders) and "Invest like the .001%: The Billionaire's Playbook" (which is about the tax-free power of Life Insurance)

If that's not enough evidence for you, pick up a copy of the best seller: "Money. Wealth. Life Insurance – how the wealthy use Life Insurance as a Tax-Free Personal Bank to Supercharge Their Savings" by Jake Thompson, 2013.

Friends, there is a reason why I own 4 fixed indexed annuities and 10 life insurance policies. You heard me right, 10!

To date, I have never had one single client complain when I have delivered a tax-free life insurance payment to them. However, I've had many people wish there had been more zeros at the end of the check. This is simply one of the greatest tools you have at your disposal to plan for your financial future. I simply cannot overstate this: Consider increasing your permanent coverage and take care of this today, while you can!

CHAPTER

9

SAFE MONEY RETIREMENT ACCOUNTS REALLY MATTER

An author named Bruce Watson told the following story. While on vacation with his young family, he came across a sign that said "Naturalist Camp." *"How cool,"* he thought, *"We'll take this trail and see nature at its best."* He soon found out what "naturalist camp" really means. Before long, six totally naked bikers came along and rode right past their entire family. Of course, the mom and dad were shocked and horrified and wondered what their kids were thinking.

Suddenly, the youngest child spoke up in an accusatory tone, "Dad! They're not wearing their helmets!"

If you're not careful as you journey through life, you can find yourself so focused on something that *seems* important that you fail to notice something that's even more important. I see this happen with retirement planning almost daily.

My dad spent his entire career in the financial services industry. Near the end of his career, he spent 17 years as an assistant vice president at Merrill Lynch. In the fall of 2013, he retired and came to work with me at my financial services company. This should be no surprise to you, but his Merrill Lynch 401(k) is no longer invested in the stock market with Merrill Lynch. His entire 401(k), which represents his life savings, was rolled over into an IRA and is now invested in a Safe Money account that pays him a guaranteed income for life

Why would my Dad, who has worked in the financial services industry his entire life, move his own personal accounts from risk to safety after spending his entire career telling people to put their money into the stock market? Why is he now telling his clients to prepare for a major stock market correction? I'll let you think about that for yourself as I tell you the following true story about one of my clients, shared with his permission.

HOW LONG SHOULD YOU WAIT?

A 65-year-old client had been listening to our radio program, "Safe Money Radio," for about a year. He knew it was near the end of his career and he planned to roll his 401(k) out of the stock market and into the safety of the guaranteed pension accounts he'd heard about on my show. He called me in December of 2013 and we started talking about all the ins and outs of doing direct trustee-to-trustee transfers of a 401(k) to an IRA and a Safe Money account. Very clearly, I told my potential client that at some point, this bull market will end; and when it does, it will remind you of 2008.

I made sure he understood that if at any point he felt the market was about to drop while he was waiting for his scheduled September 2014 retirement date, he could move from risk to safety simply by moving to cash in his 401(k) account. That would secure his retirement savings until he was ready to move to complete safety with the accounts we were discussing.

As time went on and life continued to happen, he got busy. He kept in touch and continued talking to me about the transfer, but he wasn't too concerned about the markets because, after all, they were still going up. And then late July 2014 happened. In a matter of only four days, to be exact, he watched his 401(k) drop by almost $30,000 in value.

Now this may not seem like a big deal to anyone who's played the market your whole life. After all, you've been taught not to worry about it because it always comes back. But is that advice the same when you're less than 30 days from retirement? And you need to start taking distributions from that money to live on? The answer is a big, fat *NO*.

Right now, it's estimated that almost 10,000 people turn 65 every single day in the U.S. Those 10,000 people should remember very well what happened to their retirement accounts in 2008, when they were 60. What if they experience another 2008 now? Remember earlier in the book when I mentioned the TRIPLE WHAMMY that hits retirement accounts? That's when a person who has retired has started taking distributions from their accounts, and while they are taking distributions, they experience major losses and pay fees to an advisor even though they are losing money from their accounts. Losses + fee + distributions= Triple Whammy to your accounts! That is not a formula for success in retirement. That is a formula for failure.

Let me give you a real-life example of what can happen to a successful millionaire very quickly if he goes through a 2001 or 2008 bear market at the wrong time.

4% OF WHAT?

Meet Jeff, a gentleman who, at the age of 50, opts for early retirement in 1999 with a portfolio of $1,300,000. Jeff's retirement planning has gone very well, and after meeting with his financial advisor, he feels very comfortable with his ability to stick with the plan they've made to make his money last the rest of his life. He decides to retire and try it.

With no debt, Jeff only needs $40,000 a year to maintain his current lifestyle and, after all, that's only 3% of his assets. That's 1% less than the 4% rule that keeps him from withdrawing too much of his money, so, according to their retirement analysis, he doesn't need to worry about running out of money.

Things are rocking along great at the beginning of his retirement and Jeff is enjoying life, but then something happened. 9/11 and the dot.com bubble burst happened. Jeff's portfolio dropped from $1.3 million to $800,000 in a very short period. Remember, he needs $40,000 to maintain his lifestyle. Now, withdrawing $40,000 out of an $800,000 account represents 5% of his principal instead of 3%. That was a scary time, but after several years of stock market recovery from 2002 to 2007, one of the best bull runs in market history, Jeff watched his retirement assets go back up to over $1 million.

Now his $40,000 withdrawal only represents 4% of his total assets, and he starts feeling good again about his retirement plan. Then the financial meltdown of 2008 happened. After taking his annual distributions in 2008 and in 2009, paying fees and losing almost 40% of his account value, Jeff's new IRA balance is... are you ready for this? $390,000. At this point, he decided to walk away from his then-financial advisor's plan, realizing if things continued down the same path, he would be dead broke and back at work by age 60. You see, he had hoped to become a *multi*millionaire and that didn't quite work out.

He realized he was happy with his current lifestyle and only wanted to preserve what he had, but maintaining a $40,000-a-year withdrawal from his current retirement account of $390,000 would represent 10.3% of his assets per year. Do you think Jeff had to make a major lifestyle change at this point? How do you think he felt about his retirement plan, after experiencing the losses of 2001 and 2008 from his high-risk-based accounts?

Jeff's retirement plan was shattered by the *sequence of returns*. What do I mean by that? His high-risk accounts suffered major losses *after he retired*, when he was already taking distributions. After retirement is the time when you can least afford catastrophic losses and bear markets. You no longer have the luxury of time to recoup those losses.

FORESEEING THE FUTURE—IT CAN BE DONE

There are several different lessons to be learned from Jeff's real life example.

1. If you need income from your assets, you have to respect the need for safety and make that a core priority in your financial plan.

2. The sequence of returns and risks is the single most immediate risk you face in retirement.

3. Your assets should be divided into at least two buckets: income and growth. Funds in the income bucket need to be 100% safe, conservative and protected against loss.

4. For optimum allocation in retirement, no more than 10% of your portfolio should be in equities.

Now I probably need to repeat that last one. No more than 10% of your portfolio should be in risk-based equities if you're in retirement. Taking a current look at your financial plan, you need to look at your age and the amount of money you have at risk in volatile markets. Warren Buffett widely publicizes his "Rule of 100" regarding retirement. He says to subtract your age from 100 and invest the remainder in risky equities. The rest should be 100% safe. I agree with Mr. Buffett to a degree. But today, living in a post 9/11 world, I believe you should use the "Rule of 80" that I teach in my classes.

I recommend subtracting your age from 80 and putting that remainder in volatile investments. Then and only then if you 100% comfortable with potentially losing what you have in those investments. Warren Buffett is a very intelligent man, and I endorse the following quotes from him whole-heartedly:

> I never attempt to make money on the stock market; I buy on the assumption that they could close the market the next day and not reopen it for five years.

> Only when the tide goes out, do you discover who's been swimming naked.

In other words, if you've put all your money in risky investments with no guarantees and the market drops, everyone will know it. My all-time Warren Buffett quote for investing is, "Rule number one, never lose money. Rule number two, never forget rule number one." I find it interesting that one of the wealthiest men in the world is averse to risk and losing money. If anyone has money to lose, it's Warren Buffett, and his number one rule for investing is "never lose money." In other words, my friends, when it comes to your retirement accounts, Safe Money Matters.

And if you don't believe me about the importance of focusing on SAFETY in your retirement planning, that's ok. Don't take my word for it. Let's listen to those who have gone on before us. Let's listen to someone who was born in 1874. Have you ever heard of George Clayson? George Clayson wrote a book back in 1926 that has sold more than 2,000,000 copies.

George's book *The Richest Man in Babylon* has been called "the most inspiring book on wealth ever written."

In the book, he tells the story of a young man comes into a small fortune (50 pieces of gold), and he simply doesn't know what to do with it. He doesn't want to lose it and he needs advice! So he goes to the Gold lender for advice instead of asking for a loan. You see, everyone knew the Gold Lender was rich and wise, and the young man wanted advice on how to secure his 50 pieces of Gold. As the Gold Lender spoke, he gave the young man rules regarding Gold. Listen closely to some of his advice:

Guard thy treasures from loss - "The first sound principle of investing is security for thy principal. Is it wise to be intrigued by larger earnings when thy principal may be lost? I say not. The penalty of risk is probable loss. Study carefully, before parting with thy treasure, each assurance that it may be safely reclaimed. Be not misled by thine own romantic desires to make wealth more rapidly."(Pg 44-45)

Insure a future income – "Therefore do I say that it behooves a man to make preparation for a suitable income in the days to come, when he is no longer young, and to make preparations for his family should he be no longer with them to comfort and support them...no man can afford not to insure a treasure for his old age and the protection of his family, no matter how prosperous his business and his investments may be...provide in advance for the needs of thy growing age and the protection of thy family." (Pg 49-52)

Better a little caution than a great regret – "Therefore, be not swayed by the fantastic plans of impractical men who think they see ways to force thy gold to make earnings unusually large. Such plans are the creations of dreamers unskilled in the safe and dependable laws of trade. Be conservative in what thou expect it to earn that thou mayest keep and enjoy thy treasure. To hire it out with a promise of usurious returns is to invite loss."(Pg 116-118)

The Gold Lender goes on to say "In this day, behind the impregnable walls of insurance, savings accounts and dependable investments, we can guard ourselves against the unexpected tragedies that may enter our door and seat themselves before any fireside. We cannot afford to be without adequate protection." (p.124)

This is absolutely brilliant, and is why this book has been called one of the most inspiriting books on wealth ever written. George shares 7 rules for investing in his book. Two of those rules are "Guard thy treasures from loss" and "Insure a future income."

You insure your car against the risk of loss! You insure your home against the risk of loss! Your insure your health against the risk of loss!

How many of you have insured your most valuable asset against the risk of loss: YOUR RETIREMENT ACCOUNTS! You've spent your entire life working to build up these accounts. If they are not protected against loss, you could lose up to 40% of what you've worked so hard for overnight! Remember 2001? Remember 2008?

YOUR OWN CRYSTAL BALL

I have a very important question for you, one I've asked my clients for years. Ready? Here it is. "What will happen to your retirement accounts in the future?" Can you answer this very simple question?

If your answer is "Brad, how could I possibly know what will happen to my retirement accounts in the future?" then we need to talk about your current financial plan.

If you answered, "Well, duh, they're going to go up and they're going to go down," then we need to talk about your current financial plan.

Finally, if your answer is, "Brad, based on what I see happening in this economy right now, I don't even know *what* to think about what will happen to my retirement accounts in the future," then I would definitely love to talk to you about your current and future financial plan. Why?

Every one of my clients *knows* the answer to those questions and their answers are completely different from those three. Their answers sound something like this:

> Brad, no matter what happens in this economy or in the stock market, my retirement account will never lose one penny. I have guarantees for my income account, of its growth rate every single year, and that I can never outlive the pension I receive for myself and my spouse from my retirement accounts.

If you want to know how they know that and how they got that peace of mind, then I would love for you talk to any of my clients and they would love to talk to you. I provide referrals lists with my clients' names and numbers upon request. Go to my website at www.guaranteedsafemoney.com to learn more about what I do for all of my clients. You'll learn, firsthand, what my clients have known and what they have been doing for years when it comes to your retirement money and your life savings: Safe Money Matters. Do I believe this enough to invest my own money in it? You better believe it. I opened my first Safe Money account in May of 2008. That was pretty good timing, wasn't it? ☺

I often say during my radio shows that I keep my returns in my desk in my office and I'll show them to anyone who asks. I now own 4 fixed indexed annuities and 10 specialized kinds of life insurance. The life insurance accounts will provide me and my heirs with TAX-FREE income for the rest of our lives.

Do you want to know why I believe in Safe Money Accounts? I have owned them long enough to see how they work for myself and hundreds and hundreds of clients. So let me share some of my own personal returns from my own accounts.

> In 2008, my Safe Money Account made 1.1% (Do you remember how much money you lost in '08?)

- In 2009, my Safe Money account made 20.38%
- In 2010, my Safe Money account made 6.1%
- In 2011, my Safe Money account made 8.28%
- In 2012, my Safe Money account made 5.85%
- In 2013, my Safe Money account made 11.9%
- In 2014, my Safe Money account made 5.8%
- In 2015, my Safe Money account made 6.33%
- In 2016, my Safe Money account made 7.42%

And just today, as I write this in January of 2017, my dad called to tell me he made 9.88% in his Safe Money Account.

While these returns might be appealing to you, please don't miss the greatest point about these accounts. It's not the % of return that matters the most. What matters the most is that in every single one of these accounts, I am 100% protected against losses and fees. Every single year, when I make interest in any of these accounts, that becomes part of my guaranteed value. No matter what happens in the markets after that, I cannot lose the money I have already gained. And all these accounts have guaranteed income riders attached to them that will pay me an income stream for the rest of my life, no matter how long I live. That is what matters most about a Safe Money Account.

If this sounds interesting to you, and if you would like to learn more about it, then you can listen to my show "Safe Money Radio." It can be found on my personal website, www.guaranteedsafemoney.com. And KSGF, 104.1 FM in Springfield, actually has podcasts of my radio program. If you go to the KSGF website, you can listen to archived radio programs to learn more about what you've read here..

Thank you for taking the time to read this book. I hope you've learned something about the risks of following the crowds when it comes to your retirement savings and how you can draw guaranteed lifetime income from your savings after you retire. I hope you'll choose to find a safe harbor in this storm-filled world.

APPENDIX: TIPS TO
AVOID SCAMS

In Chapter 4, I talked about the "YO-YO" economy, meaning "You're On Your Own" when it comes to finding the right financial advisor. In that chapter, I encouraged you to consider your advisor's motives when recommending financial products and services and to be aware that, just because the firm handling your finances has a well-known name, it doesn't necessarily have your best interests at heart. In fact, it may mean the opposite.

However, there are other pitfalls for the unwary investor, so it is vital for you to perform your own due diligence when looking for an advisor. Following are some tips and suggestions to help you avoid those hazards.

Perform the basics. Check out the company on the Better Business Bureau (BBB) site. See how long they've been in business, what their rating is, whether they've had complaints, and whether they've been resolved.

Make sure the individual you're dealing with is properly licensed. It's probably a good idea to Google the individual; their background may provide valuable information regarding their trustworthiness.

When rolling over funds, *never* write a check from your retirement account to an individual or his/her company. Anytime you want to move money into a different account it should be a *direct transfer.* Any rollovers I do for clients are direct, trustee-to-trustee transfers.

When rolling over funds, you can perform due diligence by checking on the institution or financial account you're moving funds *to.* Make sure it is an "A" rated company and that there is public knowledge about their financial status. If this information is not made available to the public, you do not want to do business with them.

Here is a great questionnaire for your current or potential advisor:

How many years have you been in the financial services industry? _____

Have you ever had a formal complaint filed against you with the State Insurance Department or FINRA? _____
If so, what was the result of the complaint that was filed?

_____

Have you ever personally filed for bankruptcy? _____

Do you charge fees? _____ If so, what is the range of your annual fees? _____ Do you still charge these fees if you lose my money? _____ (1–1.5% is average, up to 2% acceptable. Anything greater is excessive.)

Do you sell annuities? _____

If yes, which types of annuities do you sell and why?

Fixed Annuities _____

Variable Annuities _____

Fixed Indexed Annuities _____

(Variable annuities are fee-based annuities where you can lose your principal. With a variable annuity, the advisor still earns a commission when you lose your principal.)

What percentage of each of the annuities above do you sell?

_____

How much total premium (in millions) have you sold of the annuities mentioned above? (An advisor with reputable sales experience will have at least $10 million in active annuity production under his management.)

_____

Do you sell life insurance? _____ Why or why not?

_____

Do you have any specialized training in regard to IRA's and 401(k)s? _____

Why or Why not? _____

If yes, can I please see a copy of the material from your most recent conference/training? (If they cannot provide a recent copy of the material from an IRA training conference with the date on it, this is a red flag. IRA/401k laws change frequently and if you are working with an advisor who is not up to date with their training, there is a good chance they are giving you out of date advice. Ask to see what they are studying to stay on top of things for your tax-deferred investments and look for current dates on their study guides!)

Are you employed by a firm or are you independent?

_____

(Advisors employed by a firm are constrained in their offerings by the products and services that firm chooses to offer. This is why I feel it's important for advisors to be independent, leaving them free to choose products and services from hundreds of different companies.)

Can you represent any product/account you choose or does it have to be approved by your company?

_____

*Have the advisor sign and date this form

*Keep in mind, if an advisor is not licensed to sell you something and/or has no experience with that product/account, does it make sense to you why they would tell you that is a *bad* investment choice for you? They have no experience with it? You're in a YO-YO economy! Be smart and do your homework! ☺

About the Author

Brad Pistole lives in Ozark, Missouri with his 18-year-old son and his 21-year-old daughter.

Brad is the CEO of Trinity Insurance and Financial Services, located off Highway 65, just one block East of Lambert's Restaurant. His father Joe has joined him in the business after a long career in the corporate financial services industry. Joe has over 40 years of experience working with group 401ks and IRAs, and in helping clients achieve the retirements of their dreams. They now offer a full line of financial services to their clients.

Graduating with a BS in Education from Arkansas Tech University in 1993, Brad holds his life insurance, health insurance, and Property and Casualty (P&C) licenses in both Missouri and Arkansas. Brad is a member of the National Ethics Association (NEA), the Ozark Chamber of Commerce and the Million Dollar Round Table (MDRT), the premier association of financial professionals. He has been a member of this prestigious organization from 2011–2017 and was recognized as a TOP OF THE TABLE Advisor from 2015–2017. Brad has also been honored as a "Gold Eagle Advisor" with American Equity from 2009–2016. He was also recognized as a President's Club member in 2015–2017. This honor is given to less than 1% of all of the nation's advisors working with American Equity.

Brad has been recognized with Ed Slott and Company, LLC, as an Ed Slott Master Elite IRA Advisor. (See www.irahelp.com/find-an-advisor.) He is also the weekly host of Safe Money Radio, which airs in Springfield, Missouri, on KWTO 560 AM news *Talk of the Ozarks* and on KSGF 104.1 FM.

Brad specializes in several different aspects of the financial planning market, including retirement income planning, 401(k) and IRA rollovers, Roth IRA conversions, Social Security maximization, and tax-free retirement and estate planning through life insurance. Brad shows his clients how to use fixed and fixed-index annuities, life insurance and other guaranteed investments that will help you reduce, defer and even eliminate your taxes with no risk of principal loss, while providing you with a lifetime of income—ensuring you will never outlive your money.

Brad enjoys the outdoors and loves to run, bike, fish, and hunt. He played college golf and still plays on occasion. He spends the majority of his free time with his kids, who are very involved in choir and school activities. Brad has been very involved in mission work, coaching his kids' basketball teams, and in leadership in his local church and community.

Notes

[i] Ernst and Young LLP, July 2008.

[ii] BoBrow V Commisioner, T.C. Memo. 2014-21 and one-rollover-per year limitations of S408(d)(3)(B) of the Internal Revenue Code.

[iii] Schneider, Michael, et.al. Summer of Monuments. *Deal or No Deal.* (U.S. Game Show) from Wikipedia, the free encyclopedia. http://en.wikipedia.org/wiki/Deal_or_No_Deal_(U.S._game_show. September 3, 2014.

[iv] Mistal, Christopher. Stock Traders Almanac. "$Spy 10% Corrections in Bull Markets," May 15, 2014.

[v] __ *Investopedia.* Dictionary. Definition of "Standard & Poor's – S&P." http://www.investopedia.com/terms/s/sp.asp. September 3, 2014.

[vi] Shell, Adam, USA Today. "Down January in stocks is bad omen for 2014." February 2, 2014.

[vii] Shell, Adam, USA Today. "Down January in stocks is bad omen for 2014." February 2, 2014.

[viii] Shell, Adam, USA Today. "Down January in stocks is bad omen for 2014." February 2, 2014.

[ix] Shell, Adam, USA Today. "Down January in stocks is bad omen for 2014." February 2, 2014.

[x] Shell, Adam, USA Today. "Down January in stocks is bad omen for 2014." February 2, 2014.

[xi] Berson, Jeffrey. PRODUCERSWeb.com. *Don't listen to Suze Orman's "buy term and invest the difference.* June 24, 2013 http://www.producersweb.com/r/pwebmc/d/contentFocus/?pcID=2ed 87e21ea8dea1c2df88db8994af4fb. 09/07/2014.

Made in the USA
Middletown, DE
08 February 2017